RADIO I

Peter Mulryan was born in Dublin in 1961. He took an honours degree in Communication Studies from the NIHE, Dublin. He began work as a presenter on RTE's *Youngline* programme, then moved to Radio 2 as a reporter, before becoming a television continuity announcer and scriptwriter. Since leaving RTE, he has been involved in independent film and video production as well as lecturing in broadcasting. He now lives and works in the UK.

BORDER *line*
PUBLICATIONS

RADIO RADIO

Peter Mulryan

Borderline Publications
Dublin, 1988

Published in 1988 by
Borderline Publications
38 Clarendon Street
Dublin 2
Ireland.

ISBN No.   1 870300 03 3

Computer Graphics by Mark Percival
Cover Illustration and Origination by Artworks (Tel: 794910)
Typesetting and Design by Laserworks Co-operative (Tel: 794793)

CONTENTS

Acknowledgements

Preface by the Author

Introduction by Dave Fanning

ACKNOWLEDGEMENTS

In a book that has consumed such a large and important period of my life, I feel I must take time out to thank all those who have helped me over the years.

Since the bulk of this text is built around interviews I have personally conducted, I would like to thank those who let themselves be interviewed (some several times). They were, Roger and Ann Lloyd, Eamon Cooke, James Dillon, Robbie Robinson, Mick Doyle, Declan Meehan, Billy Wall, Mike Hogan, Andrew Hanlon, Chris Cary, Eddie Ryan, Tony Allan, Eric Graham, Eamon Brookes, Tony Boylan, Jimmy Smith, Tom Hardy, Adrian Kennedy, Sally Reynolds, David Harvey and Paul Vincent. My thanks too to Mary C. Thomas for access to her taped interviews and thesis.

Two people who granted me interviews must be singled out for a special mention. Firstly Keiran Murray who graciously gave me access to his Free Radio Campaign Ireland files and his wealth of knowledge in the area. Secondly Ken Sheehan, the original founder of Radio Dublin. Without his help this book could never have been as accurate as it is. For the proofing, wisdom and cups of tea, many thanks! I would also like to thank Bernard Evans for tracking down some of the graphics.

There were others too who assisted me in my background research. I am grateful to Bernard Llewellyn, Dennis Murray, Dion Breen, Martin Block, Margaret Nelson, Dave Fanning, Neil O' Shea, Gerard Roe, Gary Wild, Tony Donlon, and to Ruth and Barrie Johnson. I'd also like to formally thank the staff of The National Library of Ireland, BBC Northern Ireland, RTE library, the IBA in London, the NIHE Dublin library, the ITU in Geneva, the DIHE in Bournemouth, the State Paper Office Dublin, and the Department of Communications.

On a more personal level I must thank my mother for proofing the early drafts, my father for the free biros and everyone else for putting up with me.

A special debt of gratitude is owed To Fiona Sweeney, who suffered me and my various projects for so long. A 'thank you' seems hardly enough so I'll try 'sorry'.

Without a shadow of a doubt the most influential person behind this book is Prof. T.J. Wheeler (Tim to his friends!). Even though Tim moved house and college, his commitment and interest in this project never wavered. For his personal kindness, his micro, his time and friendship and his lessons in how to liberate white A4 from other people's photocopiers, I will be eternally grateful!

Finally I'd like to thank all at Borderline for their enthusiasm and commitment to this book.

P M

The author and the publishers gratefully acknowledge the following people and organisations for their contribution to this book: The Irish Times, the Irish Press Group, Robbie Robinson, Mike Hogan, Adrian Kennedy, Ken Sheehan and Dennis Murray.

PREFACE

Radio Radio is the result of six years research into unlicensed radio in Ireland. It takes the subject from the very birth of the Irish Republic in 1916, right up to the present day. Pirate stations by their very nature tend to be secretive. Like the outlaws of the wild west, station operators see themselves engaged in a battle for survival against the powers that be. These latter-day cowboys are individuals who distrust bureaucracy and conformity and indeed anything or anyone who threatens their freewheeling and therefore glamorous lifestyle.

In such a covert industry records are rarely kept, and anything documented by stations tends to be grossly biased. Facts cease to exist and are replaced by opinions. Getting to the truth then was like making a huge jigsaw puzzle on a trampoline.

In boiling down the mountain of material I have accumulated over the years, I have tried to keep the text as accessible as possible. I have avoided in-jokes, buzz words, lists of people and boring details about technical equipment. This book is aimed at anyone who listens to the radio or has had their curiosity aroused by the pirate stations.

Writing is selective and what is recorded becomes fact - whatever the reality. Memory fades, the written word doesn't. The official story of Irish broadcasting revolves around RTE. It records the organisation's successes and failures and presents them in isolation as the truth. As Orwell's Winston Smith found, "Who controls the past controls the future; who controls the present controls the past."

Pirate radio and the influence it has had on Irish society have been ignored. Contrary to the official story, unlicensed radio has been a lot more than an irritation on the backside of State monopoly broadcasting.

Because pirate stations were not bound hand and foot by legislation, during the 1970s and 80s they anticipated all the major innovations in Irish radio, like Irish language broadcasting, music radio, and twenty four hour broadcasting. While RTE was first to introduce experimental community radio, it stayed as just that - experimental. Pirate stations under the guidance of the NACB matured to meet a real public demand.

On the commercial front, successful stations invested heavily in quality mixers, optimods, transmitters and jingle packages. Professionally this put them ahead of RTE, who were struggling with the hairshirt reality of a semi-State existence.

In relation to broadcast talent, many of the present and future 'names' began life on pirate radio. Those stations were setting the trends, not only with their musical formats, but with outside broadcasting, big-money competitions, and additions to the very grammar of radio - so that MW and VHF became respectively AM and FM, while in tune with the pirate vogue Radio 2 took a second name, 2FM.

With RTE following initiatives set by pirates, the organisation lost its dominance. Unlicenced stations then grew in power and influenced the development of broadcasting in Ireland to as great, if not a greater extent than RTE.

This then is that story.

FOREWORD

It seems to me there were 3 kinds of people involved in pirate radio in the late 70s. There were those who loved the technical side of broadcasting and the excitement of trying to use the airwaves to provide a local Luxemburg/Caroline style service. Then there were those who saw it as a way to make money. Finally there were those who loved music and playing records.

I never knew much about transmitters, frequencies or modulators, and looking back on the two years I spent (between August '77 and May '79 on Radio Dublin and Big D) I never made a penny. In fact, the only way to get home from town four nights a week at 5 or 6 in the morning was by taxi (sticking 50 albums on the back carrier is not recommended!) and I was able to pay for that by working as a DJ in McGonagle's in South Anne Street at the weekends.

Radio Dublin, where we broadcast from the front room of a terraced house in Inchicore, was good fun; but my best memories of the 70s all revolve around late night Big D in '78, in Chapel Lane near Parnell Square. All we wanted was to be left alone after midnight, free of hypocritical station jingles, non-stop ads and the relentless 9-5 pursuit of profit through pop.

Myself and Smiley Bolger were in charge after midnight and nothing mattered but the music. Smiley used to arrive down from McGonagle's and start his programme at 3.33am. He'd plug in his ghettoblaster which acted as a thumping studio monitor and he'd change the light bulb from normal to red. The result? Great music, great fun.

From the midnight hour onwards the 'studios' in Chapel Lane acted as a regular visiting place for local bands who'd come along to be interviewed and get their demos played. One of those bands was U2.

In this excellently researched book, Peter states that Big D was "based in an old closed up factory with a hole in the roof. The station was always cold and damp." Factually he is right, but it was never like that when Smiley was around.

Peter has done an excellent job at making, to quote his own phrase, "a huge jigsaw puzzle on a trampoline." This is *the story* of the Irish pirates. Even if you weren't there, it's a great read.

Dave Fanning
Dublin, March 1988.

To broadcasters on both sides of the fence

The World's First Broadcast

"The Irish breed rebels where the English breed gentlemen. The English like to watch the action: the Irish provide it."
Ronan O'Rahilly, founder of Radio Caroline.

Reis' 'Fancy Goods Warehouse', on the corner of Dublin's Sackville Street and Lower Abbey Street was under heavy attack for the second day running. Over the shop, broadcasting history was in the making, but that history was probably the last thing going through the minds of the Irish rebels that Easter Tuesday, 25th April 1916.

Upstairs at 10-11 Lower Sackville Street (now O'Connell Street) was the Irish School of Wireless Telegraphy, and since occupying the building the previous day, the rebels had been repairing an old 1.5 Kw ship's transmitter. From 5.30pm that Easter Tuesday, until they were forced to leave the air at midday the following day, they informed anyone who may have been listening in to their Morse signal that a rebellion had taken place, and that an Irish Republic had been declared in Dublin. Up to this, Wireless Telegraphy had mainly been used in ship to shore communication. Here for the first time radio was used to reach a potential mass audience. The rebels were using the medium in a vain hope that some passing ships would pick up their transmissions and relay them to the United States. The rebels' message therefore wasn't aimed at any specific source; it was, in the true sense of the word, the world's first broadcast.

Although the rebels were forced off the air, they managed to smuggle part of the transmitter across Sackville Street, in an upturned table, to the GPO. All this was accomplished under a hail of British bullets.

By Friday, the GPO was in flames, and the transmitter perished in the fire. Pearse and his followers vacated the building and "...turned into Moore Street, striving to break northwards through the encircling military cordon...But Moore Street was dominated by a military barricade and The O'Rahilly, leading a forlorn charge against it, was shot down and killed." (FSL Lyons 1973, p.374)

'The O'Rahilly' was none other than Michael Joseph O'Rahilly - grandfather of Ronan O'Rahilly, who was to set up Radio Caroline almost fifty years to the day after his famous ancestor died.

•••

The silence of World War I gave way to the roaring twenties, and the tinsel generation played with their new toy, the wireless. In Ireland though, broadcasting would have to be put on the long finger as the Irish Free State was in the throes of the Civil War, a war that raged for nearly a year, from 1922 to 1923.

With hindsight, the attitude of the British government (and therefore the Irish Provisional Government), towards radio was rather utilitarian. The wireless was seen as being a tool of the electronics industry: in London, Marconi operated station 2LO; in Birmingham, Western Electric had 5IT while the Metropolitan Vickers group ran Manchester 2ZY. These companies were later to join forces to form the British Broadcasting Company.

Even as the Irish Provisional Government were monitoring the progress of the UK radio experience, the British were examining the situation in the United States of America. Here stations survived not on licence fees but on advertising revenue. This led to an early form of all-American, *laissez-faire* radio. This broadcast system led to numerous stations playing lots of jazz, something the

British Postmaster General felt would not work in the UK, " it would result only in chaos, only in a much more exaggerated form than it exists in the United States."

Shortly after this, John Reith became the British Broadcasting Company's first General Manager. He saw a monopoly of the airwaves as helping a "unified direction", and as a further means of imposing his dream of radio as being a medium which would educate, inform, and entertain. On January 1st 1927, the British Broadcasting Corporation came into existence, and under the paternal guidance of Lord Reith it grew into the centralised monopoly that inspired the Irish legislators.

Bearing in mind the social, political and economic problems facing the Free State after the Civil War, legislation onWireless Telegraphy came rather quickly. Barely three months after the first 'free' general election in the history of the State, the new Postmaster General, J.J. Walsh, presented his 1923 White Paper on broadcasting. "The combination of firms in the White Paper bears some resemblance to the BBC..." reported the examining committee. The resemblance was more than passing and the paper on *Irish Wireless Telegraphy* was to have further reaching consequences than anyone at the time could possibly have guessed.

The White Paper proposed that the Irish Broadcasting Company (IBC) would operate "a system of broadcasting in the Free State under licence from the Post Office." Five private radio companies were to run the IBC between them. One of these companies was Irish Developments Ltd., of 3 Molesworth Street, Dublin, and two of the original directors were a Mr. Figgis and a Mr. Belton. The IBC therefore was a private organisation with commercial backing. The IBC's programmes were to originate in the capital, and broadcasting hours were to be restricted to one hour in the morning, between 11am and midday, and an ambitious six hours in the evening between 5pm and 11pm.

On 14th December 1923, Deputy Darrell Figgis moved a Dail motion, "That a committee of this house be appointed to consider the circular...entitled *'Wireless Broadcasting'*, especially in regard to the proposal which...should pass over the right to license and tax incoming wireless apparatus to a clearing house under the control of a private company."

It was agreed that a ten member committee be established to discuss the White Paper and to make a recommendation on the future of broadcasting in Ireland. Deputy Figgis had started a lot more than he could ever have imagined. A former journalist, Figgis had done his bit for Ireland. In May 1914 he accompanied Erskine Childers into Germany to

> In 1922 only 0.32% of the UK population were able to listen to the radio. In seven short years the figure had jumped to over 70%.
> By 1972 there were more radio receivers than people in the US, 1,339 for every 1,000.
> *(Council of Europe 1977)*

purchase arms for the 1916 rebellion. While on this mission Childers got the inspiration for his famous espionage novel *Riddle of the Sands*. In the early twenties Figgis dabbled in business before going into politics. It was during this period that he met Andrew Belton, a local entrepreneur, and together they set up Irish Developments Ltd. That company was one of the five constituent members of the proposed Irish Broadcasting Company, and Figgis was on the Dail committee discussing the future of Irish radio.

When Figgis' involvement with IBC's Belton became public, there was an outcry from furious TDs and an irate press. It was alleged that Belton was paying his old partner for political favours. Although Figgis strenuously denied the charges of corruption, the controversy raged, and on January 25th 1924, Figgis resigned. In his letter of resignation, Figgis explained that although they were once partners, had thoughts of helping Belton through political influence "been present to my mind, it is unnecessary to say that I certainly would not have accepted nomination to the committee." Amid all the scandal and uproar, a second member of the IBC Deputy Sean MacGarry resigned, due to his connections with the electrical trade. The effect of the Figgis-Belton affair on the final recommendations of the committee can never be measured. At this stage the whole future of Irish broadcasting lay on a knife edge: to one side State control, private commercial interests to the other.

State control means just that. The broadcasting station is either a branch of the civil service, or is linked to a government department, i.e. Communications. The content of the station is controlled by legislation. This ensures 'social responsibility', broadcasting in the public interest and trying to please all of the people some of the time.

Commercial or independent radio can be different. In the US and Australia, stations are left to their own devices. Within the laws of decency, stations can broadcast what they will. Market forces and not State control dictate programme content. So stations tend to cater for demographically targetted mass markets, with music. This is not only cheap to produce but guarantees a specific, usually young audience, and this keeps advertisers happy.

Commercial broadcasting can however have elements of Public Service Broadcasting, as with Independent TV and radio in the UK. But this compromise rests uneasily as paternal State control and the realities of the business world are poles apart. Ireland then was at a crossroads. Would the committee accept the White Paper and the commercial IBC, or would they follow the British model of State control?

The unsavoury commercial overtones of the Figgis-Belton affair were undoubtedly among the factors that tipped the balance in favour of State controlled radio. Brash commercialism, it would seem, left a nasty taste in the mouths of the committee members: "...of the firms or individuals named in the White Paper as constituent units of the proposed Irish Broadcasting

Company...one at least has only the interest of a financier in the exploitation of broadcasting." No prizes for guessing which company they were talking about!

Lord Thompson was years later to speak of commercial broadcasting as "a licence to print money". The IBC were never to experience Lord Thompson's enjoyable cliché. It was felt that the early history of Irish Developments Ltd. was "such as to convince the committee that the broadcasting concession should not be extended to that company."

With Irish Developments out of the race for a licence, the very foundations crumbled from beneath the IBC, and the White Paper was certain to be rejected.

What was left of the committee issued their final report on 26th March 1924. It recommended, quite simply and bluntly that "broadcasting should be a State service purely - the installation and the working of it to be solely in the hands of the Postal Ministry." There was to be no commercial radio. The decision to recommend State control was taken because of the committee's belief that radio should be used for other purposes besides entertainment. It was felt that radio should be used to educate, to teach languages, and to impart the wonderfully rustic trio of "...fruit-growing, bee-keeping, and poultry-raising"! They also felt that radio was of national importance and therefore any entertainment value was "quite subsidiary". In 1923, they may have had a point.

In the early twenties the wounds of the Civil War were far from healed. The population was split pro- and anti-Treaty. The Free State was in political turmoil. Economically the State was sinking into a depression. 1921 to 1923 was a time of economic crisis, with agricultural prices dropping weekly. Therefore the Provisional Government felt that any medium that could encourage good farm husbandry and promote a unified national spirit should be exploited, not for private commercial gain but for the greater good of the citizens of Ireland: radio was that medium, and the State was to control it.

The Dail began debating the committee's report two days after its submission on 28th March, but the recommendations weren't accepted until 7th May, and then only after a heated debate. On one occasion, the Postmaster General, J.J. Walsh, summed up his feelings on the subject, "I am assured that the ordinary user of receiving sets feels that anything else but music jars on his nerves."

The debate outside Leinster House though was just beginning, and as the decades rolled by the voices of those who felt Ireland needed commercial broadcasting were to grow louder and louder as the State monopoly floundered like a beached whale.

The First Pirate

While the government was still trying to find potential operators to run an indigenous Irish radio service, private enterprise stepped in in the shape of the Marconi organisation, who already operated a successful radio station in

London. It was Horse Show week, August 1923, and Marconi had a microphone and a transmitter situated in the Royal Marine Hotel, Dun Laoghaire, while the receiver was some six miles away in the Royal Dublin Society's showgrounds, Ballsbridge. For many Dublin people this was to be their first taste of Wireless Telegraphy. They marvelled at the twice daily broadcasts and the news bulletins provided by the *Evening Mail*. But the experimental station was short lived. On Thursday morning, 17th August, the station failed to appear on the air. It had been closed down on the orders of the Postmaster General. This is how the *Evening Mail* of the day reported the story:

"The temporary station at the Royal Marine Hotel, which aroused such interest and admiration has now been dismantled and the instruments taken out of the country at the request of the Postmaster General."

It was to be a taste of things to come, private enterprise taking upon itself to supply a service not provided by the State and the closure of that enterprise by representatives of the State.

•••

That station from the Royal Marine had aroused much public interest, and shortly after this Irish newspapers started publishing tuning guides to UK stations. Slowly the amount of people fiddling with 'cats whiskers' and crystal sets began to grow. By 1924 advertisements for wireless receivers had become quite commonplace, promising "Nights of Pleasure: Opera, Dance Music, Songs, Lectures and the Late News at your command every night!" However as there were still no stations operating in the Free State, listeners had to make do with an imported culture.

On 27th May 1925, the government finally published its plans for the future of broadcasting in Ireland. It was J.J. Walsh, Minister for Posts and Telegraphs (his title had changed from Postmaster General in 1924), who made the announcement. Ireland was to have State controlled Public Service Broadcasting, and the first station, 2RN, was to be on air for New Year's Day, 1926.

In the months leading to the launch of the station, excitement began to grow in the capital. Newspapers carried articles explaining exactly what radio did, how it could travel without wires for miles right into the living room, even with the windows closed!

At 7.45pm, 1st January 1926, the airwaves crackled into life, "This is 2RN, the Dublin Broadcasting Station calling!" Then Dr. Douglas Hyde, later to become the Republic's first President addressed the nation:

"Our enterprise to-day marks the beginning not only of a new year, but of a new era, an era in which our nation will take its place among the other nations of the world...While not forgetting what is best in what other countries have to offer us, we desire to especially emphasise what we have derived from our Gaelic ancestors, from one of the oldest civilisations in Europe, the heritage of the O's and the Mac's."

Although the Dublin press gave excellent coverage to the launch of 2RN, the *Cork Examiner* was unmoved. After all, the station was for Dublin, and audible only within twenty-five miles of the transmitter in McKee Barracks. 2RN was meant to be the start of a string of localised stations around the country. Cork would follow, then Galway, Waterford etc., "thus using the talents of the whole country, for the whole country," said J.J. Walsh.

However his committment to this kind of broadcasting is questionable, because in July 1926 as the British Broadcasting Corporation was being planned, he announced plans to build a national transmitter in the midlands.

By 1929, the numerous British stations had joined forces, moved to London and become the centralised monopoly of the British Broadcasting Corporation. Ireland too adopted this model. Cork, the country's second city, enjoyed its own station 6CK for a short three and a half years. On 30th September 1930 it closed. Although Cork was later to become the centre of local TV and radio opt-out (*) broadcasts, the closing of 6CK was the end of regular decentralised broadcasting in Ireland.

The Dublin station 2RN now found itself being rebroadcast in Cork. Then in 1933, when a powerful new 60Kw transmitter was opened in Athlone, the station could be heard all over the country. By 1937 Ireland had three transmitters in operation. The powerful Athlone rig, the power of which had been increased to 100Kw, and smaller transmitters in both Dublin and Cork. All three broadcast the same station, and by March 1939, this radio service became known as 'Radio Eireann'.

* The process whereby a regional station leaves a national network and broadcasts its own programmes for a limited period.

7

Below are highlights from two programme schedules for January the first. One is from the opening night of 2RN in 1926, the other from Radio Eireann in 1966. After forty years the programmes are not only interchangeable but almost identical. Can you tell which is which?

1st January 19XX * ·

6.20	pm	Announcements
6.45	pm	A commemorative programme on the Easter Rising in 1916
7.30	pm	Gaelic Songs
8.01	pm	A programme featuring a prominant Irish comedienne
9.01	pm	A recording of a Classical music recital
10.30	pm	Ceili Music
11.30	pm	Light music and songs

1st January 19XX *

7.45	pm	Announcements
8.00	pm	Number One Army Band plays Irish Ballads
8.15	pm	Gaelic Songs
9.15	pm	Irish Pipe Music
9.35	pm	Classical music from Chopin and Field
10.05	pm	A selection of Choral music
10.20	pm	Tristan and Isolde

The similarities are striking. Even eleven years after the latest of those two schedules, on 1st January 1977, the only change was a one hour 'Discs-A-Gogan' from 7 to 8pm presented by the perennial Larry Gogan. This tokenism wasn't good enough. Clearly RTE's finger wasn't on the pulse of Irish life. In a country with such a young population, is it any wonder the pirates became so popular so quickly?

•••

In 1960, 'Radio Eireann' became Radio Telefis Eireann' (RTE), as the organisation took onto itself the provision of television broadcasting as well as radio. With this departure RTE ceased to be a branch of the civil service and an authority was appointed to take over responsibility for the station's running. However RTE was still a semi-State organisation and it suffered from all the

---

* The first set of programmes is from 1966, the second from 1926.

problems associated with a slow-moving bureaucracy, complacent in its monopolistic cocoon.

While the years passed and new technologies like Direct Broadcast Satellite and Cable came on the scene, the legislative base of Irish broadcasting remained basically the same as it was in 1926. The broadcasting environment in which RTE operated had changed drastically, yet legislation failed to keep pace with these changes. By the 1980s, RTE had not only to compete with four British television channels, home video recorders, satellite TV and a host of British radio stations, but also with up to one hundred native pirate radio stations, that legally shouldn't have existed.

RTE continued to provide a nation-wide service, though by the early eighties the organisation found it increasingly difficult to maintain standards. The radio and television channels, its orchestras, its mobile radio studios and ever rising costs were slowly strangling the State monopoly. "The cash situation is getting worse by the day" warned John Sorohan, the chairman of the station's management association, while in 1982, Fred O'Donovan was even bleaker on the future of RTE, "we cannot hope to embark on anything but survival - this is now a survival operation."

As the RTE bureaucracy became ever more cash starved, it became ever more centralised. A gap was left for a local radio service. This gap was filled by private entrepreneurs. So pirate radio in Ireland grew largely because and in spite of RTE, thriving on the very deficiencies in the State controlled service.

Legislation

It was November 1926 before the Dail debated the long awaited 'Wireless and Telegraphy Bill', but the legislation made a quick passage through both houses and by 16th December 1926, it had become law. The 1926 Act defines Wireless Telegraphy thus:

"'Wireless Telegraphy' means and includes any system of communicating messages, spoken words, music, images, pictures, prints or other communications, sounds, signs or signals by means of radiated electro-magnetic waves originating in an apparatus or device constructed for the purpose of originating such communications, sounds, signs, or signals."

For 1926 this definition was quite comprehensive, and makes reservations for the eight month old innovation called television, even though at the time television was given little chance of catching on. Much of this Act is concerned with ship-to-shore communication. Sections three and eight concern us most closely.

Section three is concerned with "Restrictions on possession of Wireless Telegraphy apparatus." It is stated that **"no person shall keep or have in his possession anywhere in Saorstait Eireann, or in any ship or aircraft...appara-**

tus for Wireless Telegraphy save in so far as such keeping or possession is authorised by a licence granted under this Act." It then goes on to tell us that anyone who does possess such transmitting equipment "shall be guilty of an offence...and shall be liable on summary conviction thereof to a fine not exceeding ten pounds, together with...a further fine not exceeding one pound for every day during which the offence continues and also, in every case, forfeiture of all the apparatus in respect of which the offence was committed." In 1926, £10 was equal to half a night's broadcasting budget on 2RN, but by 1980 £10 wouldn't even buy a single forty five second spot on Radio Carousel. Timelessness is not a quality Radio Acts possess in abundance. This Act has other qualities too, like a lot of loopholes.

Section two of the Act defines an "apparatus for Wireless Telegraphy", or transmitter, but the definition is qualified with the statement that the apparatus must "not (be) capable of being conveniently used for any other purpose". Subjective words like "conveniently" don't belong in pieces of legislation. All that's needed is that proof be presented that indeed the transmitter does have other convenient uses besides transmitting and the case has to be dismissed. In March 1977, Eamon Cooke, owner of Radio Dublin successfully fought off legal action when he demonstrated that his transmitter could be put to other uses besides transmitting. At this time Radio Dublin had been in operation in one form or another for eleven years. Commenting on the courts' ruling on his transmitter, Cooke stated that, "...because of the fact that it could possibly be used for other things bar transmitting, the case was dismissed." But even when the pirate stations were caught broadcasting, fines were paltry.

Radio Melinda was another station to run foul of the law. In this case a two pound fine was imposed on the broadcasters in 1973. Ten years later Robbie Robinson was fined only £20 for operating Sunshine Radio, a station with an annual turnover of several hundred thousand pounds!

Ridiculous as these incidents sound, they are just proof of how weak the 1926 Act actually was. The sections dealing with pirate broadcasting were unable to weed out the initial Irish hobby radio stations. So, in the absence of any strict laws prohibiting unlicensed stations, the pirates grew in size and in sophistication. As the number of pirate stations mushroomed in the 1970s, all Jack Lynch, the Taoiseach, could say was that they "...can be a source of acute embarrassment to this country internationally." Lynch had got his facts backwards. The pirates were not the cause of the embarrassment, the pirates were not the cause of anything - rather they were the symptom, the symptom of the frustration felt by commercial and community interest groups. The frustration that springs from hopelessly inept legislation. By choosing to play it safe and take no legislative action against the pirates, the governments themselves became the first to disdain the law. So they led by example. Maybe that is the most embarrassing fact of them all.

2

Freedom
and
Choice

"There is something irresistibly romantic about a ship wallowing lazily in a light swell...and a small team of technicians and disc jockeys defying state monopolies...to take programmes into the homes of millions."
Paul Harris, broadcast historian and writer.

In the Europe of the 1920s and 1930s, the radio world was a lot less complicated than it is to-day. One by one the European governments licensed regular broadcasting services. Britain led the way with the inauguration of the British Broadcasting Company in 1922. A year later, in 1923, the Swiss, the Germans and the Belgians licensed their broadcasting organisations. They were followed in 1924 by Austria and Finland,

and finally in 1926 the Irish joined their European neighbours, with the setting up of 2RN.

In the beginning then, each State controlled its own limited air space. There were few frequencies on which to broadcast and a large population with diverse tastes - Public Service Broadcasting (PSB) was born and with it the notion of 'social responsibility'. Here the Broadcast organisations tried to strike a balance between the shortage of available frequencies and the need for truly comprehensive programming on limited resources. The aim of individual plurality from a centralised monopoly gave the world PSB.

However as time went on more and more frequencies became available to the civilian broadcaster, equipment became less expensive and lighter. By the 1960s then as transmitters became more powerful, signals travelled further and national boundaries meant nothing, the State monopoly of the 'national airwaves' had become something of a myth. Radio Luxemburg and a host of pirates were booming across Europe, as people tuned in to the alternatives.

Initially, European countries found themselves in an ideological dilemma. On the one hand these democracies had to be seen to be in tune with public opinion, and on the other they had to protect the State monopoly of the airwaves. Freedom of speech was pitted against the protectionism of social responsibility. On one end of the 'freedom' spectrum lay anarchy, on the other authoritarianism. In profit-oriented western democracies governments found it harder and harder to ignore the public demand for a broadcast alternative - a choice. The cries of 'press freedom' grew louder and louder, and since any notion of press freedom means a plurality of channels and ideas, by definition it tends towards the anarchic end of the spectrum. Keeping the State broadcasting monopoly and excluding private concerns could be seen as a denial of freedom, something the 'free world' is conceptually opposed to.

Western governments found themselves at the centre of this difficulty, and with true foresight they chose to ignore the problem in the hope that it would go away. Problems however never do so, and while the State broadcasting monopolies did their competent best, their ideological and bureaucratic structures began to buckle under the weight of commercial pressure.

Robbie Robinson, a seasoned broadcaster from both licensed and unlicensed radio, put it succinctly. "There's no way that any one (broadcast) organisation can satisfy the needs and varied tastes of a nation." This train of thought is nothing new. As far back as 1946, Sir Frederick Ogilvy, an ex-Director General of the BBC warned in a letter to *The Times,* "Monopoly broadcasting is inevitably a negation of freedom; no matter how efficiently it is run, it denies freedom of choice to listeners."

This is true. But there is no sense of 'public responsibility' in commercial radio, and a greater number of stations does not *automatically* lead to greater choice. To put it bluntly, commercial radio is not a charity, it is out to make a profit. The community radio lobby, on the other hand, seldom have the contacts or the financial backing to win political favours, while those interested in 'Free Radio' long for an ideal world that does not exist, whereby stations are allowed to operate free from any external, political, commercial or union pressures. Moreover, commercial interests nurture 'Free Radio' as a handy smokescreen to hide behind. Back in 1966 during the height of the UK off-shore radio pirates, a leading London newspaper wrote on the subject of pirate radio, "If the government is viewing the stations with increasing disfavour, the advertising community is not...We regard them as a serious means of advertising", a leading advertising agent told *The Times*." So the men with the money threw their considerable weight behind the 'Free Radio' lobby. As we will see this also happened in Ireland. Without these financial godfathers, the Irish stations could never have survived, let alone prospered. Their presence assured a proliferation of 'free' commercial pirates in the monetarist eighties.

The Off-Shore Radio Phenomenon

The mini-skirt was in, Beatlemania was sweeping Britain, and off the European mainland pirate radio ships were broadcasting a new kind of sound, to a generation born to the affluence of the sixties. Off-shore radio became a reality for the first time in 1958 when 'Radio Mercur' began broadcasting to Denmark. All in all there had been no less than eleven off-shore stations in operation before Ronan O'Rahilly's Radio Caroline came on the air, but most of these stations had been closed by 1964 when the relevant countries passed legislation to prohibit the pirate operators.

When Caroline arrived on the scene there were still two radio ships braving the elements and broadcasting. They were Radio Syd off the Swedish coast and Radio Veronica off the coast of Holland. The latter station became the first offshore pirate to broadcast in the English language, when it started a daily service in April 1960. British off-shore radio piracy came into being on Easter Sunday 1964. The station was Radio Caroline and with it came a totally new sound, that of independent commercial radio. Radio Caroline operated from the 'Fredrica', originally a Dutch ship that O'Rahilly had renovated at Greenore Harbour.

At this stage the BBC still enjoyed a monopoly over the native British radio waves. The BBC did not cater adequately to the tastes of youth. Moreover, the BBC had to abide by restrictive 'needletime' agreements, which controlled the amount of music from disc that could be played over the air. These restrictions imposed by the Musicians' Union meant that in 1964 the BBC could only play 75 hours of disc music in a 374 hour radio week. The remaining 299 hours had to be filled with taped music the BBC had commissioned, or with idle banter by presenters. Of course 'needletime' restrictions didn't apply to the pirates, much

Ronan O'Rahilly

The original Caroline
in calm waters

to the joy of the British public. The sixties had begun to swing, but the official airwaves hadn't. Around London there had grown up a proliferation of 'Beat Clubs', playing to a generation that had never experienced a World War, a generation craving excitement. It was to this audience that the pirates were to appeal.

The Caroline Connection

Ronan O'Rahilly was an idealistic young Irishman who had emigrated from his native land to the UK after being thrown out of secondary school. In London his determined personality soon had him earning his living touring the beat clubs and acting as agent to many musical unknowns of the era. One of O'Rahilly's more promising acts was Georgie Fame, an as yet unknown pop singer. O'Rahilly was having problems getting the artist any air time, the BBC were smugly complacent, and most of the air time on the independent station Radio Luxemburg had been bought up by the major record companies, EMI, Decca, Phillips and Pye.

The monopoly in the record industry was just another symptom of the hold a small number of organisations had over the broadcasting system. O'Rahilly felt that the BBC gave the public what it thought they wanted, and therefore it didn't answer a real public need. Auntie Beeb reserved valuable air time for culture with a capital 'C'. Ronan was frustrated. He felt the only way to solve the problem was to set up his own radio station. "I wanted to break that monopoly, so I started Caroline. I knew that if Caroline died the monopoly would grow." But Radio Caroline didn't die, and in common with a lot of the later developments in the pirate radio world, it turned out to be a lot more successful than anyone at the time could have guessed. In the first three weeks of operation, Caroline built up an audience of seven million people, a truly phenomenal success.

It's worth expanding on what happened after Radio Caroline took to the air. Firstly because there are many amazing parallels between the British pirate experience and that of the Irish, and it was on board Caroline and the other off-shore pirates that many of the later gurus of Irish radio piracy were to serve their apprentice-ships. As Caroline was preparing to take to the sea and was being fitted out north of Dublin, another pirate, Alan Crawford's Radio Atlanta, was also preparing to take to the air waves. The race was on to make it first, and on 29th March 1964, Radio Caroline started broadcasting, *"Hello everybody. This is Radio Caroline broadcasting on 199, your all day music station!"*

On 9th May, Radio Atlanta also commenced broadcasting from the 'Mi Amigo', from an anchorage within sight of the Caroline ship. Atlanta broadcast on 200 metres, right on top of the Caroline frequency, and initially the station would open for transmissions when Caroline shut down for the night. By 29th May a third pirate station set sail, but unlike the previous two stations, Radio Sutch occupied an abandoned Army fort at Shivering Sands, in the Thames estuary.

It was on 2nd July that the most exciting radio news yet broke - Radio Caroline and Radio Atlanta were to join forces under the Caroline banner. The 'Fredrica' was to continue broadcasting from its present anchorage off the South coast of England, and that station was to be called Caroline South. The 'Mi Amigo' was to sail north and anchor off the Isle of Man. It was to be Caroline North.

Over the following months station after station set sail, fanned on by the success of the Caroline organisation and by the continual head-scratching of the government in Whitehall. At this stage the pirate operators were not illegal. Under the British Wireless Telegraphy Act

By 1965 there were between 120 and 300 companies registered as willing to operate commercial radio stations in Britain.

Of all the abandoned army forts occupied by the pirates, only one was outside British territorial waters. Rough Towers, off the Essex coast was occupied in 1966 by Roy and Joan Bates, who promptly renamed the fort 'Sealand' and declared an independent Republic. Although a constant thorn in the side of the British Government, Prince Roy lived, relatively untroubled, on the fort for twenty two years. Then in 1987 Roy announced he was offering six radio and TV franchises. At the same time Britain increased its territorial limit from three to twelve miles, thus swallowing up Sealand. Prince Roy simply felt the whole thing was "very exciting"!

of 1949 the buccaneering broadcasters were totally outside existing laws, they were extra-legal, and in the swinging sixties this gave the pirates the only legitimacy they needed.

It took three years to draw up the necessary legislation to sink the pirates. On 13th June 1967, the British Parliament passed the "Marine Broadcasting (Offences) Act", which when given the Royal Assent became law, and the swashbuckling days of the pirates were numbered. The date for the implementation of the new Act was the 15th August 1967. After that date, any British subject working on a pirate ship would be liable for prosecution. As June and July dragged by, petitions to save the pirates were circulated. But in the end the lists of names were to prove largely useless. The pirate stations prepared to leave the airwaves; all that is, but one - Radio Caroline.

After 15th August 1967, it took some time for Caroline to get back into full swing. The station moved its headquarters to Amsterdam, while a smaller office was established in Dublin's trendy Grafton Street. From the Irish office George Hare would deliver records, letters and wages to the floating ship. But just when things were picking up, disaster struck. The two Caroline ships were boarded and towed back to dry land. What happened to Caroline lay in the splitting of the ownership between O'Rahilly and Philip Solomon, a highly secretive businessman. In an effort to maximise profits, Solomon gave precedence to getting money into the organisation at the expense of giving it out. The debts mounted, until finally the salvage company, Wijsmuller, who were owed money by the Caroline organisation, could hold off on payment no

Robinson and Cary in their Caroline days.

longer. So with writs nailed to the masts the two Caroline ships were towed into harbour. The 'Fredrica' (Caroline North) was broken up for scrap, and the 'Mi Amigo' (Caroline South), lay rotting in an Amsterdam harbour. The Caroline organisation though was far from inactive, and the 'Mi Amigo' was eventually re-floated. On 22nd December 1972, Radio Caroline again opened shop.

• • •

The teenagers of the nineteen sixties grew up, and the economic recession of the early seventies brought any remaining hippies back down to earth with a bang. All this time Radio Caroline continued to broadcast with almost indestructible will-power. Then in 1979, when it seemed that this eternal teenager would continue forever, the 'Mi Amigo' sank below the waves. Radio Caroline was no more.

No sooner had the radio ship reached the bottom than rumours of yet another phoenix-from-the-ashes began to circulate. The rumours persisted with the Caroline organisation saying that the station "...will defiantly return....". And all over these islands Anoraks* continued to tune up and down the dial in eternal hope, waiting for the second coming. Caroline finally returned on 15th August 1983, on the anniversary of the implementation of the Marine Broadcasting (Offences) Act, 1967.

Life on the open sea is far from easy. It's cumbersome and expensive. Chris Cary has described off-shore radio piracy as "a barbaric way to broadcast". When there is an easy way to do something clever businessmen do it that way, and if Chris Cary is anything, he's a clever businessman. Unlike Solomon, Cary feels that

* An 'Anorak' is a slightly derisive name given to a 'Free Radio' enthusiast. The nickname comes from their favourite item of clothing.

After 15th August 1967, any British subject working for a pirate radio station was liable for prosecution. To get around this Major Barker Solomon took out Irish citizenship. Only two British disc jockeys remained with Caroline after 15th August. They were, ironically enough, Spangles Muldoon (Chris Cary), and Admiral Robbie Dale (Robbie Robinson), who were later to found Ireland's first superpirate, Sunshine Radio.

Philip Solomon

"..anybody in this day and age that starts up a pirate radio station on a boat must have brains missing."

In early 1980 Philip Solomon was planning to re-float Caroline. He had interested a group of businessmen to the tune of several million pounds. Solomon then contacted an old friend from his Radio Caroline days. His job was to explore the validity of the project and to acquire a suitable ship from which to operate: that friend was Robbie Robinson. But the plans to re-float Caroline never materialised. The reasons are numerous and doubtless include Cary's discovery that Ireland was rather lenient on radio pirates. This discovery led Solomon and Cary to invest in Sunshine Radio. The coming of the professional British pirate operators was essential to the process of streamlining the nation's rather staid pirate broadcasters. With professionals like Chris Cary, Robbie Robinson and Tony Allan came experience and capital. The British radio pirates had made Ireland their new radio ship.

Tony Allan and Martin Block, two of the British talents who were to improve the quality of broadcasting on the Irish pirates.

3

Fusewire,
Black
Coffee
And
True Grit

"Pirate radio? The popular image now is probably one of rain sodden, mud splashed anarchists crouched in the corner of a remote field with a black box, a long piece of wire and a car battery."
John Marshall, *Broadcast Magazine.*

The *official* history of pirate radio in Ireland is terribly uneventful and unexciting. It revolves around the opening and closing of transmitters. But the real story of Irish radio during this period is a lot more exciting. This time belongs to a few pioneers, radio enthusiasts who built and operated small transmitters simply for pleasure.

The Pirate

The beginnings of radio piracy have become lost in the mists of time. Unlicensed or pirate radio preceded the Irish State broadcasting system, and exists, or has existed in just about every nation on Earth.

The first Irish pirate of any significance was political, and operated during the Second World War, or euphemistically, 'The Emergency', since Ireland was neutral. The pirate would come on air from suburban Dublin 9/11, at ten past nine at night. The broadcasts would begin "Churchill means hunger and war!" His identity, though suspected, was never proved. He was of course a Nazi sympathiser, and rebroadcast the famous Radio Hamburg propaganda of William Joyce, better known as Lord Haw Haw because of his upper class British accent. In January 1946 Joyce was shot for treason. His body lay in a quicklime grave for twenty years until he was reburied in Galway, where he had once studied to be a Jesuit. Nothing as unpleasant as this was to happen to his mysterious sympathiser. After ten minutes the transmissions would end with the enigmatic phrase: "This is a workers' challenge calling!"

The Colleen Home Service

Tony Boylan's love of radio stretches back to the days when, as a boy, he would build his own crystal sets and listen in on foreign broadcasts. The Boylan family lived in Colleen Road, Rathmines. Tony's father was in the army, and at that time anyone found in possession of a radio transmitter could have been accused of "collaborating with the enemy". But to young Tony thoughts of prosecution were far from reality. In 1944 he opened his first station, 'The Colleen Home Service', but his father forced him to close it down! Not one to take defeat lightly, Tony hid his home made transmitter beneath the floor-boards.

After 1946 Tony built up a fairly constant listenership. His audience were mainly neighbours, but he received many record requests from as far afield as Cork Street hospital! Don't forget these were the days of large, black and very fragile 78s, when record players were hand cranked, when electricity was a recent innovation and the paraffin most people used to light their homes was still rationed. Boylan was the only radio pirate operating in Ireland. In fact the term 'pirate' hadn't even been thought of as yet.

By the early fifties Tony had built a new transmitter, and extended his broad-cast hours to include some Saturday programming as well as his regular Sunday lunchtime transmission. During this time Tony was never contacted in any way by the Department of Posts and Telegraphs. However, when he increased the power of his transmitter and the reception radius extended over twelve miles, his new station, Radio 200, ran into trouble with the Department.

Fearing a raid Tony closed down voluntarily, but not for long. He was soon back on a new frequency and with a new name, Radio Laxey.

Shortly after this Tony moved house, to the northside suburb of Ballymun. Here he started 'The Ballymun Home Service' which broadcast every Sunday morning for a number of years. Then Tony moved house again, down the road to Santry, the site of his most successful station, Radio Galaxy. It was the early 1960s and around Europe off-shore radio piracy was finding its sea legs. In Dublin the hobby radio stations were about to become very popular, and the Department of Posts and Telegraphs were once more on the trail of the radio pirates. One bright Sunday morning Radio Galaxy started broadcasting, as it had done now for several years. No sooner had Tony begun broadcasting than a white volkswagen car drew up outside his house. Two officials from the Department got out and walked to the front door. They were refused entry and after twenty minutes of banging and shouting, they went away.

That afternoon Tony Boylan smuggled the transmitter into the boot of his car. He intended hiding it until the pressure from the Department eased off. At 4.50 pm that evening Tony and his wife drove out of their house. They were to get five o'clock mass on the Airport road, and then dispose of the transmitter. No sooner had they left the driveway than Tony noticed a white car tailing them, and inside it were the Post Office engineers: in true heroic style Tony panicked, put his foot down, and sped off up the road, pursued by the white Volkswagen. In the subsequent chase Mr. Boylan lost the two engineers but got flagged down by the Gardai for overtaking on a white line. Tony explained that he was in a hurry to get to mass. The Gardai let him go. About four months later Tony Boylan brought Radio Galaxy back into regular service with a forty watt transmitter, and in his own words "...I

Pirate radio has always been important to political activists. In the Europe of the thirties the 'Freedom Station' broadcast anti-Nazi propaganda and was ruthlessly hunted down by the Gestapo. The Algerian resistance used radio extensively. Franz Fanon wrote:" *The radio has become just as necessary as arms for the people in the struggle against French colonialism.*"

never had any further visits from them." The Department of Posts and Telegraphs had clocked up their first defeat.

Tony Boylan and his various stations plodded along during the 1940s, 50s, 60s and even into the seventies. In 1972 the Galaxy transmitter was brought back into service for Radio na Saoirse (Radio Freedom). At the time Ireland was debating whether or not to join the EEC. This station spoke out against it, but the message fell on deaf ears and on January 1st 1973, Ireland joined the European Economic Community.

Tony Boylan's pioneering broadcasts were amazing feats of personal and electronic achievement, and they were well ahead of their day. While Tony proved that pirate radio was technically possible, it would take younger men another ten years to prove its economic feasibility, and they were still at school.

●●●

Young Davitt Kelly operated his station from the family flat in Dublin's fashionable Mount Street in the middle sixties. The transmitter was homemade from bits of a Philips radio, complete with a little dial that would glow (as would Davitt) whenever it went on air. Radio Atlantis, or Karina, or whatever Davitt decided to call it when he got up in the morning, had one problem - no record player. Davitt hadn't got around to building one. But necessity being the mother of invention, he soon had the problem sorted out. Davitt simply relayed Radio Luxemburg through his transmitter and interrupted whenever he felt the 208 disc jockey was about to speak! Then one morning there was a knock on the door. The Department of Posts and Telegraphs had traced Davitt's station - he had been raided.

Several months later, when the case came to court, Davitt's father was fined the princely sum of two pounds for letting a station operate from his house. Davitt was fined one shilling. However in true arch-villain style he had skipped the country for the summer, returning in the autumn with armfuls of records he'd got while fixing juke boxes! That winter Davitt threw in his lot with Jack O'Carroll of Radio 66, and Radio Jacqueline was formed. This station was to prove one of the most consistent of all the hobby broadcasters in the years ahead.

The Shape of Things to Come

Modern Irish radio piracy has its roots in the Dublin of the early 1960s. It was at this time that the first of many hobby radio stations started transmitting. Programmes tended to be brief, limited to a half hour or so on a Sunday morning. At this stage little or no attention was paid to programme content, it was enough to have made a broadcast. Transmitters tended to be home made and power ranged from five watts for a small station to around forty watts for a station of reasonable size. Broadcast fidelity was poor and the received signal from a pirate station was of telephonic quality, in that sound was often warped and distorted. But the early radio pirates were driven on by pure determination. Soon station operators were all known to each other, radio broadcasting was almost like a club, and a transmitter was your ticket of admission.

By the 1970s stations were mushrooming all over the capital. Station names, locations and frequencies changed so often that today a lot of the details have been forgotten, even by the station operators. One thing though is still crystal clear in the minds of the early hobby pirates, and that is the fun and excitement they felt as they ran their stations from attics, basements and spare bedrooms. James Dillon, who went on to operate his own station, The Big D, remembers listening in to these early broadcasts. "It was the type of situation that if you moved your radio a little more to the left than the right, you lost the station completely...They were on the air, but no-one was listening!" Radio was rough and ready and stations were often held together with no more than fusewire, black coffee and grim determination.

The roots of Radio Dublin can be traced back to a station called Radio Blachliatha which Ken Sheehan operated from his house in Drimnagh in 1966. Ironically it was Davitt Kelly who first got Ken interested in broadcasting and Ken remembers his early broadcasts were "experimental", he being more interested in the ideological than the disc spinning side of broadcasting. Radio Blachliatha operated on 217 metres (a popular pirate frequency) on Sunday mornings, initially playing pre-recorded programmes made by a friend of Ken's, Roger Lloyd. Ken kept broadcasting, erratically, through the late '60s and eventually re-named his station Radio Dublin. By 1969/70 the early stations like Radio Romeo and Radio Santa Monica had, along with the ha'pennies and farthings, disappeared. In their place though were new stations, for example Eamon McGovern's Radio Eamo and Jack O'Caroll's Radio Jacqueline - they were soon joined by Tony Boylan's Radio Galaxy, making one of its periodic appearances. These three stations along with Radio Dublin set up the 'United Stations Network'.

The idea was simple. The stations would broadcast on a rota system each Sunday, one pirate coming on air after another. This way broadcast hours could be extended and some continuity could be brought to the separate operations. The idea was tried for a few weeks, but it never caught on. The first of many attempts to unify the pirates had failed. Station operators, it would seem, valued their freedom too highly. Even though no formal organisation ever unified the radio pirates, there have been countless informal relationships between individuals in stations. Radio was more a club than anything else, and Ken Sheehan refers to the early pirates as "a circle of friends".

In the cellar of Gloucester Place Mr. Tom Callandar and his raiding party found something very interesting, or even embarrassing, it depends on your point of view. It was a photo taken of Callandar and a colleague sitting in their little white VW Beetle, staking out Billy Ebrill's Radio Caroline in Dalkey. Billy had noticed the car on a few occasions and suspecting burglars had crept up to the car and flashed a quick photo of the startled P and T employees! Mr. Callandar, not renowned for his sense of humour was not impressed, and even less so on finding a copy of the photo in the Melinda studios.

By 1972 there were about half a dozen hobby stations operating in Dublin. In addition to Declan Meehan's Vanessa, Billy Ebrill operated his own Radio Caroline from Dalkey, there was John Ryan's RadioNorthside, Dermot Blake's Radio Valerie and Radio Melinda, from the Gloster Diamond, Sean MacDermott street.

In the winter of 1968 Davitt Kelly was involved with Radio Jacqueline. At the time they were experiencing interference on their 217 metres frequency. Davitt paid a visit to Ken Sheehan and asked would he "loan, swap or sell" the Radio Dublin crystal for 253. Ken lent the crystal, so for a while Radio Jacqueline operated on 253 metres. But Ken began to lose interest in broadcasting, so he passed on the rig to Roger Lloyd who operated the station from his flat in Crumlin. Whatever the problems associated with running a radio station from a house, operating Radio Dublin from a flat became next to impossible. Flats are always cramped, but with all of Roger's broadcasting equipment, things were getting out of hand. There were batteries, bits of aerial, fuse wire and of course the bulky transmitter. Add furniture and Mark Storey who was giving a hand and there wasn't even room to swing a cat's whisker, never mind a cat.

Around this time other stations began to appear on the Dublin dial. In 1970, Radio Vanessa operated from a bedroom in Santry. The room was Declan Meehan's and he was helped by his pal Robbie Irwin. Declan remembers that Radio Vanessa was named "after a girl up the road who we thought was gorgeous!" There must have been something in the northside air, as both Declan and Robbie were neighbours and often played on the road directly outside Tony Boylan's house.

The Radio Melinda Affair

After experimenting with the forty watt station Vanessa, Declan Meehan wanted to spread his wings he remembers, "because we were so interested in Radio Caroline we had to have our own station." Other people who were to be involved in that larger station were Mark Storey and Ernie Melia. As was the vogue at the time, the station was given a girl's name, Melinda.

The Melinda Seven (*Evening Press*)

This fashion started with Radio Caroline. O'Rahilly christened his station on a transatlantic crossing. In an in-flight magazine Ronan read an article on Caroline Kennedy, daughter of US President John F. Kennedy. There was a photograph of Caroline, she looked so fresh and cheerful, she summed up exactly what O'Rahilly felt his station should stand for. No-one now remembers who Radio Melinda was named after, or even if there was a Melinda, but either way the station officially opened in 5 Gloucester Place at 11am on September 9th 1972.

Just three months later the station was raided on the morning of December 17th. Seven people were charged in the basement studios. Declan Meehan, who was on air at the time of the raid had jokingly remarked that they would fight anyone who threatened to raid them. The reason he made that comment lies with the second person to be charged, Ken Sheehan. For a while Ken had suspected a raid by the Gardai, and although he had nothing to do with the station he had gone down that day to warn them. He was too late, and so the ill-timed comment from Declan. Other people charged included Michael Lynch, Jimmy Lynch, Ernie Melia, Mark Storey and Jimmy McCabe.

The court case took place on Wednesday 3rd February 1973. It is memorable on several accounts. Firstly because of the disproportionate coverage the case was given in the press. The *Evening Press* of the seventh gave the story front-page coverage and by the eighth the *Irish Independent* was referring to the tiny 50 watt station as "Radio Melinda International"! Secondly Justice Breathnach fined five of the seven accused the paltry sum of two pounds each. Finally, the charges against Michael Lynch were dismissed because he was not in the station at the time, he was on the ground floor. The charges against Ken Sheehan were upheld, even though he had no involvement in the station and the case against Mark Storey was dismissed. His summons had been mislaid.

● ● ●

On Wednesday August 22nd a new station started to test broadcast on 224 metres, beside Radio Ulster. The station, Radio Empathy, was the brainchild of Ed McDowell. By September 9th, the pirate had moved to the clearer frequency of 222 metres, where it stayed. On 3rd October, Empathy officially started broadcasting between 1pm and 3pm. By the seventeenth the station was on FM. With Empathy came a new dimension in pirate radio - regular broadcasts on medium wave and innovative FM. The station was also the first pirate to give a postal address, 31 Common Street, North Wall. After a while the address changed to the more prestigious postal residency of 59 Lansdowne Road, Ballsbridge. By Feburary 1974, Radio Empathy was undoubtedly the most powerful radio pirate in the country with an estimated output of 150 watts. In 1974 the station was still experimenting with FM* on 98.8 MHz, and broadcasts continued regularly each Sunday. By April 1974, Empathy was the jewel in the crown of Irish hobby piracy, the station was going from strength to strength, when suddenly it was raided.

On Saturday 6th April 1974, Radio Empathy went off the air in the middle of the Ed McDowell show. The transmitter was confiscated as was nearly all the electrical equipment; they even took Ed's teddybear. The other pirate operators ran scared. For the remainder of April and into May, June and July, not one single pirate station came on the air. It seemed that the jackboot tactics of the Department had worked. Irish radio piracy was dead.

After the raid on Empathy the pirate radio scene went very quiet. In August 1974 Radio Dublin drifted back on the air. At this stage Dermot Blake became involved in the station. The Radio Dublin operation had been shifted from Roger's cramped flat to Dermot's house in suburban Drumcondra. With this move to the north side transmissions began once more, much to the interest of Don Moore.

* FM, Very High Frequency is the band on which Frequency Modulation (FM) broadcasting takes place. In radio terms, the FM band between 88 MHz and 108 MHz is reserved for civilian broadcasts. FM radio had only recently come into vogue as it permits a high-fidelity signal, in stereo if necessary. FM transmitters are also extremely portable and light. This and the fact that FM signals do not travel far makes it an ideal medium for local radio. However the top end of the band is used by the Gardai and emergency services.

Dermot's sister worked with Don's then wife, Debbie Moore, and it was through this connection that Don became involved in pirate radio. With his powerful and domineering personality Don was soon in the process of taking control of Radio Dublin. After the Empathy raid, no-one dared go back on the air, although Radio Dublin did make the odd appearance in late 1974. In early 1975 Declan Meehan blew the dust off the Radio Vanessa transmitter and made the occasional broadcast, but not much happened until March of that year.

On 1st March 1975, Radio Dublin returned, though this time with a difference. That difference was Don Moore, broadcasting under the name Dr. Don. At 1pm that day Dr. Don announced Westside Radio on 225 metres. Don stayed on the air for an hour and on leaving, Roger Lloyd (Prince Terry) started broadcasting on the old Radio Dublin rig announcing "Big D, on 253." Don had all but shifted the control of the nomadic Radio Dublin from the hands of Roger Lloyd. At this stage the station had moved yet again, this time to Don's house in Cabra. As Declan Meehan remembers, Don had promised a free house, "...a home with no parents or anything like that."

• • •

By mid '75 the Dublin pirate scene was in full bloom. Coincidentally in May of that year RTE launched Radio Liberties, the organisation's first experiment in local community radio. The mobile studio used was nicknamed 'Wanderly Wagon' by those in the pirate radio world. Around this time too there was much celebrating as Ed McDowell was reunited with his kidnapped teddybear!

The Irish Radio Movement

The Irish Radio Movement (IRM) largely grew out of Ken Sheehan's disillusionment with the radio world. 1972 had seen Ken caught in the Radio Melinda case, and consequently he more or less pulled out of Radio Dublin. In 1973, along with radio enthusiast John Dowling, Ken set up the IRM.

The IRM was to be a platform for discussion and comment on the 'Free' radio scene. All aspects of radio were open for debate through the movement's publication *Medium.** Although Ken and Co. managed to move a few copies of the magazine in shops like Peats of Parnell Street, membership of the IRM, at 50p a year (the price of two pints!) never exceeded sixty. The expensive membership cards lie idle to this day, in a box under Ken's bed.

---

* No.4 of *Medium* said: *One of the main objectives of the IRM is to campaign for, and give publicity to, alternative radio.*

Standing back row l to r: Declan Meehan, Paddy Brennan, Eoin Mc Donagh
Seated centre row l to r: John Dowling, Mark Storey, Ken Sheehan, Eamonn O'Connor
Foreground: Stevie Hand

In the fourth edition of *Medium* (late 1974), the IRM published a letter from the Department of Posts and Telegraphs, setting out the official line on who was allowed to broadcast in Ireland:

> "A Chara,
> Please refer to your enquiry about the pos-
> sibility of establishing a local radio station in
> this country.
> The legal position is that under Irish law a
> single public corporation - Radio Telefis
> Eireann - is responsible for the control and
> operation of Irish broadcasting. There is no
> provision for the establishment or operation
> of broadcasting stations by private interests.
> It is not possible, therefore, under existing
> législation to grant to any person or organisa-
> tion, other than Radio Telefis Eireann, a
> licence to establish or operate a broadcasting
> service in this country.
> Signed: D. Hogan"

There you have it, short and sweet!

1974 saw the near annihilation of Irish pirate radio following the raid on Empathy. To most people it seemed that the IRM was flogging a dead horse. The movement survived the lean years of 1974/5, but apart from a vigorous letter writing campaign, its accomplishments were few and by 1977 the IRM, like the hobby stations it grew from, had vanished into the ether.

In May 1976 Radio Dublin made known details of its "Local Radio Campaign". On the second of the month the station announced that 1,850 signatures in favour of independent local radio had been collected. Radio Dublin were to host a march to Dail Eireann to take place on Saturday June 12th.

By the beginning of June Radio Laxey was back on 217, Capitol Radio was on 220 metres, a new station, Premier Radio was operating on 222 and of course Radio Dublin was on 253. This rather hectic pirate activity, plus the 6,000 signatures now reported to be collected, pointed towards this march being more successful than anyone might have expected. On the Tuesday, Wednesday, Thursday and Friday preceding the march Radio Dublin came on the air advertising Saturday's big event, saying that 100,000 signatures had now been collected!

Everyone waited for Saturday.

At 1pm on Saturday 12th June 1976, the Radio Dublin Free Radio march started. The crowd was a little down on expectations. The attendance figure wasn't 100,000; nor was it 6,500; nor 1,850 - in fact only a handful of people walked on the Dail that day. Ken Sheehan remembers that he "felt like a right twerp," as no doubt did the other twenty people who watched Dr. Don present a garda with an application for a licence to broadcast. With that the handful scattered to the pub for a drink.

The Divine Trinity

The official story behind Alternative Radio Dublin (ARD) as told in the ARD souvenir special goes as follows: "The daddy of them all Dr. Don was one of the founders of ARD back in 1975. It was at his home in Cabra that weekend broadcasts took place..." In fact Radio Dublin operated from Don's house in 1975. ARD didn't arrive on the scene until the summer of '76, and when it did it wasn't Don Moore who was behind the station, but Mark Storey, Declan Meehan and Davitt Kelly, The Divine Trinity.

Mark had been involved in Radio Dublin since the days when Roger Lloyd was in charge. But Mark didn't like what was happening to the station, and he didn't get on too well with the station engineer, Eamon Cooke. So with Davitt, who'd been living in Spain for a while, and with Declan, he set up an alternative to the existing Radio Dublin, with the predictable name of Alternative Radio Dublin (ARD).

Just prior to the founding of ARD, Mark and Declan had become involved with yet another RTE radio experiment, Radio Trinity. The station operated out of Trinity College, Dublin (where Mark was studying law), over the Whit bank holiday. This experiment was to give Declan and Mark their first taste of professional radio, experience they were to put to good use in ARD.

On July 31st 1976 ARD put out a test broadcast on 217 metres. By Friday August 6th, the station was renamed Radio Cleo, and operated on 218 metres. The two DJs on air that Friday were Arno St. Jude (Meehan), and Tom Bell (Davitt). By the 22nd of the month the station had reverted to its original name, ARD. The station however soon began to lose its sense of direction. Declan Meehan remembers "we went through various phases of being the album station, the black music station, the country station..." and so on. But even at this stage the one thing that separated ARD from the rest of the herd was their professionalism.

Over the following months Radio Dublin was to extend broadcasting hours even further. ARD, on the other hand, broadcast short yet snappy programmes. At ARD it was quality, not quantity that got precedence. During the month of September, the rivalry between Radio Dublin and ARD was just getting underway when suddenly Radio Dublin was raided. ARD had taken the precaution of coming on air after Dr. Don. This way the Department would concentrate on the first pirate signal picked up and, in theory, would leave ARD alone. So far it seemed to be working.

On September 15th, the Department raided Dr. Don's house in Cabra at around midday. But they failed to get the transmitter. Eamon Cooke had buried it in the back garden. So two days after the raid Radio Dublin were back on 227 metres explaining what had happened. DJ Keiran Murray remembers that it was "a moving broadcast". Notice was also given that for the present at any rate nighttime transmissions were being suspended. When Radio Dublin came back on air on October 3rd, a watch was being kept for Departmental activity. A Posts and Telegraphs lorry was spotted that afternoon, and at 4pm the station closed. No more was seen of the lorry. By the middle of the month most of the shock had worn off, but a watch was still kept during broadcasts.

As 1976 drew to a close, Radio Dublin extended its broadcast hours further and Dr. Don got quite a coup by interviewing Marianne Faithfull on November 14th. Christmas '76 came and went with Radio Dublin broadcasting on 253 metres, ARD on 215 and Premier on 222. The year was now 1977 - the most important year ever in the development of Irish pirate radio.

ARD gets raided - Bernard Llewellyn in the suit with the
bearded Dr.Don.

*"If it's fun and games, OK, no better man for
fun and games than myself. We can play... we
researched raids...the way Post Office men
kick."*
Eamon Cooke, owner Radio Dublin.

Conflict lies at the heart of every human
endeavour and radio is no different. Out of the
cosy club of hobby radio came ambitious people
who believed that solely to make a broadcast
shouldn't be an end in itself, rather it could be a
business enterprise. By 1977 this philosophy had
been taken on board by several Dublin enthusiasts. For them broadcasting had become an
obsession and in Dublin, the world's biggest vil-
lage, being first and best was all that mattered.

In February 1977 Radio Dublin introduced a new format. Up to this, in common with most of the other hobby pirates (the exception being ARD), Radio Dublin had broadcast golden oldie after golden oldie, the simple truth being that stations could not afford new records! But on February 6th, Radio Dublin introduced a new format of DJs playing disco music. This, along with their extended broadcasting hours marked an important development in the history of Irish radio. Unfortunately for the new DJs the schedule soon hit a major snag, another raid.

Only a week after the new schedule was introduced, on February 13th, Radio Dublin closed down twice. At 2pm transmissions came to an abrupt halt due to a raid scare and the station closed once more at 5.30pm. Everybody connected with the station was tense. One week later Radio Dublin again took to the airwaves, this time though a small precaution had been taken to confuse the Department of Posts and Telegraphs. The main Radio Dublin transmitter was still in Don Moore's house in Cabra, but a second rig had been installed at Eamon Cooke's in Inchicore. In the event of a raid scare the second transmitter was meant to be turned on. This would hopefully confuse the Department and save the main 253 transmitter. That afternoon, the twentieth, the Department raided Moore's house. The trick hadn't worked. Don's nerves were getting worse.

The next Saturday, Don went to the General Post Office in Dublin's O'Connell Street. At 2pm he covered his clothes in petrol and set himself alight. Don Moore sat there smouldering for several minutes until two units of the Dublin fire brigade put him out. The next day DJ Paul Downey officially closed down Radio Dublin: 253 fell silent.

•••

In late February 1977, Radio Clive changed its name to Radio City. The station wasn't to stay on the air for very long. On May 4th the station was raided. The police didn't have to travel very far - Radio City was next door to the Crumlin Garda Station!

•••

Radio Dublin had already made several test transmissions from a number of locations in Ballyfermot, Clondalkin and from Eamon Cooke's house in Inchicore. Eamon had been doing some standby broadcasting in the event of Don Moore's home being raided and a new Radio Dublin transmitter had just been built. Eamon kept this transmitter in his house. For a while now, relations between Eamon and Don had been strained. Two ambitious people in the one small station was too much, and following Don's fiery stunt in the G.P.O. the

Radio Dublin operation was moved from Cabra to Eamon's house. Keen rivalry brings out the worst in people, it rouses our deepest emotions. In the unregulated limelight of pirate radio, there was only ever room for one ego.

The Sunday of the move, Don Moore turned up outside Eamon's terraced house ready to open Radio Dublin, but Eamon wouldn't let him in, saying that it may have been Don's station, but it was his transmitter - therefore it was Radio Dublin from Inchicore, and Don's services were no longer required. It was May 29th 1977 and Radio Dublin broadcast from 1.45pm to 5.00pm on 253 metres, with some ex-Premier disc jockeys borrowed for the occasion.

Don was not to take his departure from Radio Dublin as the end. By the first weekend in June there were two Radio Dublins on the air, Eamon Cooke's station and Dr. Don's station, which he operated from his house on an old transmitter. Don referred to his station as Old Radio Dublin implying it was the original. His operation broadcast from 2.15pm to 7pm on 254/5 metres. Eamon Cooke however operated from 1.45pm to 6pm with new DJs Jimmy Day, Alan King, Jimmy St. Leger, Sylvie, and some jocks from Naas, who travelled up to do their shows every Sunday.

The next day, June Bank Holiday Monday of 1977, the two Radio Dublins broadcast with more or less the same format as used on the Sunday. Cooke announced that he had received 150 phone calls of support from people. His station played disco music while Don played the more traditional Radio Dublin diet of golden oldies. Both stations continued for a couple of weeks until June 12th, when Dr. Don turned up on ARD's doorstep, the same day Radio Dublin closed down at 3.30pm for fear of a raid. With Cooke in sole command of Radio Dublin, his stubborn personality was free to express itself. On June 19th, Radio Dublin broadcast an 'election special', noteable for one major fact. The station remained on-air for twenty-four hours non-stop. It therefore became the first Irish radio station, licensed or unlicensed, to do so.

Don finally decided to close Old Radio Dublin and join up with Declan, Mark and Davitt who were operating ARD from a shed in Drimnagh. "This new station is going to be the biggest thing in the history of Irish Free Radio," said Don Moore as ARD went back on air on July 31st. Initially the three were "a bit wary of Don", but an agreement was reached and ARD moved out of Davitt's garden into Don's living room in Cabra. It took a long time for the ARD crew to pull together. Initially Mark, Davitt and Declan kept broadcasting in their own right with Radio Pandora on 208 metres, while at the same time planning ARD with Dr. Don. But Pandora was raided on June 19th and Declan went to Radio Dublin for a short spell. It was to be a long while before ARD would hope to challenge the mighty Radio Dublin, which over the August Bank Holiday broadcast special programmes. They began at 2pm on July 30th, and went right through to 2am August 2nd 1977, a total of sixty hours non-stop broadcasting.

Up until Christmas 1977, Irish pirate radio stations had been, without exception, primitive. As a rule transmitters were home made and tended to broadcast more static than signal, the worn records and fluffy needles completing the inferior sound. Then in late '77 Radio Dublin installed a superior transmitter. It was still home-made, built by Billy Ebrill, but it was of a superior quality, and for once a pirate signal didn't sound like one. Reception of Radio Dublin over the capital was excellent and most people could pick up the pirate as clearly as they could RTE. The telephonic quality was gone, and so was the old format.

In these days of MTV, Music Box and Sky Trax, it's hard to appreciate just how refreshing Radio Dublin actually sounded back in early 1978. Daytime reception of foreign radio stations in the capital was fairly hopeless: there really was only Radio Eireann, with its paternalistic and static diet of programmes. Then all of a sudden there was an alternative! Chatty personality DJs playing plenty of music!

On the one day James Dillon, Mike Eastwood and Gerry Campbell all joined Radio Dublin. On November 27th Marty Hall began his career on Radio Dublin. Today he uses his real name, Marty Whelan. And on December 20th another new jock, Jason Maine, started on ARD. With all this new talent it's not hard to see why Radio Dublin took off like a bomb. In fact Eamon Cooke was so convinced that only Gay Byrne commanded a sizeable audience for his mid-morning show on Radio Eireann that when it finished, Radio Dublin would welcome back its listeners who had been tuned to RTE!

Things in pirate radio were easy going. DJ Keiran Murray remembers his first broadcast on Radio Dublin as being typical. "John Clarke had just finished his programme and there was nobody else to go on. Yours truly was hanging around, answering the phones at the time, and Eamon sort of said to me, 'would you like to go on and take over?' I was very nervous about it!" But Keiran did go on, and found himself coming back every Sunday.

At 8am on Christmas Eve 1977, Radio Dublin started its marathon Christmas broadcasting schedule. Programmes were to continue non-stop until Wednesday 28th, over one hundred hours of non-stop transmitting. DJ James Dillon remembers the factors that made this schedule possible, "...between the fact that most guys were on holidays and it was coming up towards Christmas, it seemed like a good idea to go on and broadcast all day, every day, right up to the New Year. So that's exactly what we did...The advertisers wanted to know at that stage as well." It is impossible to estimate the audience of Radio Dublin that Christmas. But the new programming, plus the new transmitter, meant for certain that more people than ever before became aware of the station's existence.

The public reaction to Radio Dublin's Christmas blitz on the airwaves was amazing. Like Caroline before it, the station had tapped a new market. No longer were radio enthusiasts the only listeners to pirate radio. James Dillon remembers that "...for the first time people started listening in shops, offices, factories, and we couldn't believe it...before if one person rang in from Santry, like everybody was leaping around the place; 'somebody in Santry heard us!!'...and all of a sudden...the line was jammed, you'd give out the number and people would say, 'I've been trying to get through for three hours'!".

On New Year's Day a triumphant Eamon Cooke broadcast his Station News. Here he thanked the Lord Mayor of Dublin, Michael Collins, for appearing on the station. He also thanked the press for all the good publicity. He thanked the listeners and the staff, with, as we shall see, an ironic 'thank you' to one DJ in particular, "My thanks to Frank Murray...for making that (broadcast) possible, many, many, thanks Frank Murray." The Captain also announced new broadcasting hours. The station was to operate from 8am to 7pm on weekdays, with non-stop broadcasting all weekend. This sort of schedule had never been tried before, by any Irish radio station. Up to this pirate operations were trotted out during a Sunday lunchtime; it was a bit like walking the dog, but less energetic.

The Elements

Going into 1978 Radio Dublin was sitting pretty. It had unparalleled broadcast experience, a large talented staff, at this time including Mike Eastwood, James Dillon, Neil O'Shea, Marty Whelan and Dave Fanning. With this talent, the larger transmitter, and extended broadcasting hours, all the strands interwove and Radio Dublin ceased to be a hobby station and became a fully commercial venture. The station accepted advertising and sponsored programmes (as did RTE Radio until 1981). Prior to Christmas of '77 Radio Dublin had been a hobby affair characterised by irregular broadcasts. There was no commitment to audience, or to advertisers. As 1977 drew to a close advertising revenue began to trickle in to the station from the odd innovative company, like the Red Corner Shop and the Angel Boutique chain owned by Noel Kirwin. Potential advertising revenue was responsible for bringing in the new transmitter. With this increase in power came a larger catchment area, and therefore more potential advertisers, all bringing in money - the life blood of a radio station.

The new disco DJs were proving very popular with a young audience bored with RTE. "The format was more or less non-stop music," recalls James Dillon, "with plenty of requests, the more requests the better, because it meant you kept one person happy when you played a request for them." There were in fact so many requests that DJs would often interrupt songs to hear their own voices and utter immortal lines like, "...this is for Derek from guess who?"

At the time, hobby broadcasters looked on Radio Dublin as an extension of Cooke's eccentric personality. Many felt that broadcasting seven days a week was a sure sign of insanity. Ken Sheehan recalls that it "...was just sheer folly, madness really, it would require a very special kind of individual to make his home a broadcasting station." Roger Lloyd also gives Cooke the credit for putting pirate radio on the map in Ireland, he was in Roger's words, "*a very courageous man*". Over the next few months Eamon Cooke was going to need all the courage he could find, as his world disintegrated around his ears.

ARD

ARD marked its first step in the battle for the loyalty of listeners with a change of frequency, from 217 metres to 257 metres. Declan Meehan remembers that 257 was chosen "...because it was exactly next door to Radio Dublin". At this stage Radio Dublin was still calling the shots and all ARD could do was follow. By late '77 advertising had begun to come to ARD. Unlike Radio Dublin, ARD openly canvassed potential advertisers and so it was that Don Moore walked into Bernard Llewellyn's electrical shop in Phibsboro one morning in September 1977. This is how Bernard tells of his first involvement with the station: "I was approached to advertise on ARD. I was then working in the retail business. Through advertising on ARD I realised that there was a need and demand for some sort of local radio service; I therefore approached the people involved in ARD with various ideas I had and which they accepted."

Llewellyn's involvement in ARD marked the first commercial backing received by an Irish pirate radio station. In return for a 50% share in the station, Bernard supplied Don with a car and a sum of money. "But," recalls Declan Meehan," it wasn't Don's station to sell." Dr. Don had, in fact, jilted Davitt, Mark and Declan in more or less the same manner that he had been sold out by Cooke. Before Bernard's involvement, the three lads had a 25% share each in the station, with Don Moore owning the remaining 25%. Afterwards the three were left "...with really nothing", recalls Declan.

In January 1978 Bernard Llewellyn injected a large sum of money into ARD. The station moved out of Don's council house and into a Georgian building at 42 Belvedere Place, near the city centre. The station was officially launched on the twenty third, with a reception in a Dublin night club. With ARD's very first broadcast it became obvious that the station was to be run in a business-like manner. While Radio Dublin continued their ad-hoc schedule, ARD spruced up their act with tight programming and snappy jingles. In fact the DJs were privately patronising, even contemptuous of Radio Dublin.

Under Llewellyn's watchful eye advertising rate cards were drawn up and printed, and a professional recording studio was used for commercials. At this time too Bernard hired Belfast journalist Ray McGuigan to run and plan programming. Under McGuigan's direction, the station started a range of innovative shows. There was daily current affairs, a woman's programme and a local news service that was widely respected. But creative programming costs more, and soon ARD was feeling the pinch and cutting corners. While minority interest and talk shows are more expensive than the musical variety, they generate the same or even less revenue. The conflict between good intentions and harsh economic reality is nothing new, and Llewellyn found he had to rethink his programming policy and opt for more music. This prompted Mark Storey, in a bitter letter to a Dublin magazine, to comment that community interest shows on ARD "are allowed to continue because they are good to point to on the programme list and say 'look how committed we are!'" By February 1978 Mark, along with Davitt and Declan had become so disillusioned with life in Belvedere Place that they left ARD, the station they had founded.

August 1977 saw the founding of Radio Clonmel, the first of the new breed of pirate stations, to be set up outside Dublin. This short-lived station broadcast on Sundays between 2pm and 8pm on 220 metres.

The Turning Point

The rise of Radio Dublin from a weekend hobby station to a small commercial enterprise had been viewed with distaste by the Department of Posts and Telegraphs. When Eamon Cooke announced that a Free Radio march was to take place on January 21st, it all became too much. The following three weeks were to prove the most eventful in the history of Irish radio.

On Tuesday January 17th 1978, six days before the launch of the new look ARD and four days before the march, Radio Dublin was raided. This was the first raid on the station since going commercial. At approximately 7pm several uniformed gardai, under the direction of Detective Sergeant John McGuire, and investigators from the Department entered the Radio Dublin studios in Inchicore. They searched the premises for transmitting equipment and in what the Captain remembers as the most vicious raid ever, record decks were turned over, tapes and papers were scattered and "..they broke windows and hurled a brick through an upstairs window".

The men continued their senseless rampage until 7.08pm when they presented a search warrant, took the transmitter and left. However Cooke had taken prior measures to ensure that any raiding party took as little as possible. On hearing the alarm, the homemade transmitter was quickly broken down into unrecognisable junk. Some parts would even be put into plastic bags and suspended off the ball-cock in the toilet, "most of the time they couldn't take anything because there was nothing there to take," remembers Cooke. "It was in little bits scattered 'round here, there and everywhere!"

The following is an extract from Detective Sergeant McGuire's official statement on the Radio Dublin raid of January 17th, "I approached the front door of number 3 Sarsfield Rd with Sgt. Riordan. Having knocked at the door it was partially opened by Mr. Eamon Cooke, who was known to me as being the owner of the house. Mr. Cooke attempted to close the door in my face, but I entered the hallway taking Sgt. Riordan with me. Sgt. Riordan signalled to Det. Sgts. McLoughlin and Hynes who were outside on the roadway. I went immediately to the rear groundfloor diningroom, I heard a noise from the room immediately upstairs as if a number of people were moving about. I saw a wire leading from the record deck in the front sittingroom to a hole which obviously led to an upstairs room. I also saw a door leading from the rear diningroom...this door was locked and bolted on the side away from me and I was unable to open same. Sgt McLoughlin who in the meantime had gone to the rear garden of the premises unlocked the bolt on this door and I ascended the stairway. I entered the bathroom and saw a man washing his hands, and whom I now know to be Mr. William Sargeant (Sarge). I made another search of the rooms accompanied by Mr. O'Neill and Mr. Dempsey of the radio section, and I lifted floor coverings in the small hallway outside the upstairs rooms and saw a loose floorboard which I lifted and saw a piece of radio equipment and two other pieces of equipment. I also took possession of the two turntable record decks from the front sittingroom and later gave same to Mr. O'Neill."

In his written statement Det. Sgt. McLoughlin who 'opened' the back door explains how he accomplished this: "The backdoor and window which gave entry to a small kitchen had notices warning of 'High Tension Wires' and 'Beware Danger'. Inside the glass panel in this door I saw bare wires about six inches apart. I found a length of timber and with this I broke the glass in the door without touching the wires. On entering the kitchen I found another locked door with a glass panel leading to the bottom of the stairs and also crisscrossed with wire and a warning notice. Again I had to force the glass panel and release the bolt..."

From these Garda statements the term 'raid' might seem to be an exaggeration. In fact these terms make a raid sound positively civilised. A more accurate 'picture' of the devastation caused by a raid can be seen in the photo on p. 49.

When the raiding parties left, it didn't take much to get a station back on the air. There were always several transmitters, in different stages of construction, stashed around the place. A couple of hours and some creative electronics later, and the station would be back to normal. The total cost of a transmitter was only a few hundred pounds and with Cooke's backing from advertisers like Tele-Rents, the Captain could afford to run the gauntlet. In true buccaneering style, within five hours of that vicious raid the Captain had Radio Dublin back on the air. The record decks were broken, which resulted in the background music for Station News speeding up and slowing down. The Captain sounded very tired and weary as he explained what had happened and that he had not wanted trouble but after that raid "...war it seems to be!" Cooke also announced an extension of broadcasting hours. Radio Dublin was to defiantly stay on the air until the following Saturday. Cooke concluded his news with a message to his listeners (and one must speculate, a dare to the Department) "Well you have Radio Dublin back!".

The following day saw The Captain splashed over all the newspapers. "10% RTE - 90% us," is how Cooke summed up his audience statistics, "but judge for yourself. Go into any shop, pub, boutique or factory and hear what's on - it's us!"

The morning of the twenty first dawned bright and clear - by two o'clock, O'Connell Street was blocked by over two thousand young people waving banners and scarves. Then the march snaked its way southwards towards the Dail, broadcasting as it went. Although Ken Sheehan was ensconced in O'Dwyer's during

The evening of the seventeenth, ARD closed down saying it feared a raid. The Department were indeed due to visit ARD after they'd returned from Eamon Cooke's - but how were ARD to know? Strict as security was at Lyon House, Dr. Don had a mole. As the raiding parties left, the" Contact" would ring Don, who promptly shut down or hid the good transmitter, replacing it with a museum piece which the Gardai would carry away in triumph! Such contacts were nothing new. In the seventies the 'Engineer" built many of the early transmitters, and he too worked for the Department!

the march, he did drop in on Eamon Cooke that night. He can clearly remember the Captain lying draped over a table in the half light. On sensing Ken, Cooke looked up and with a wry smile said, "this is the happiest day of my life!"

So it was that Radio Dublin remained on the air for four days non-stop, directly following a raid, and as the direct result of that raid. By the end of January, broadcasting hours had been extended even further, with Dave Fanning's 'Rock Show' taking the station up to midnight. On January 25th, the Radio Dublin aerial was cut down by The Department. That same day ARD closed down due to 'technical difficulties'. It was just over a week since their last visit when it was noticed that the cheeky Cooke was using telephone poles to support his aerial. A Department memo takes up the story:

memo:

"It is gathered that the poles are not in use by the Post Office...in my opinion we would be open to the charge of being reckless if we simply cut the wires loose from the poles while Radio Dublin is on the air. Radio Dublin would claim that there was high voltage on the aerial wires and that people who might come in contact then would be in danger of electrocution. Accordingly it will be necessary to raid or visit again at the time of disconnection of the aerial wires and hopefully removal of the pole. I use the word visit because I feel any appearance of the law accompanied by personnel at Mr. Cooke's door would automatically lead to disabling and dismantling of his transmitter. The visit could be for the purpose of checking whether he has a licence for his TV set. Three TV sets were seen in his house. Removal of poles will not put Mr. Cooke off the air, but it will mean that he has a much inferior aerial and that signal strength and range will deteriorate accordingly. He will reconnect the aerial unless the poles are removed".

A week later the Radio Dublin aerial was knocked down. They never asked to see Eamon Cooke's TV licence!

On February 11th, a fortnight after the felling of the Inchicore aerial, the station was again raided. At 6.10pm, four or five men came to Cooke's house. A new reinforced door had been fitted since their last visit, so they stuck their heads through the open studio window! Eamon Cooke saw them and ran to disconnect the transmitter. After about twenty minutes the men left empty handed; they hadn't even gained access to the building. If they had seized the transmitter Radio Dublin could well have been silenced, as there was no standby rig to bring into service. No sooner had the men left than 'The Captain' came on air to announce that the station was to broadcast around the clock until that Sunday.

On March 18th 1978, Radio Dublin announced that it was about to commence twenty four broadcasting, every day.

Not only did the Department's raids fail to rid the airwaves of the pirates, but they encouraged the growth of these stations. Eamon Cooke remembers "..three raids in succession within three weeks and still we were back, and there was no great fuss, nobody was off and locked up...they searched for equipment and they went away again, we went back on the air and they came back again!" The Department's failure to control Radio Dublin gave the green light to other pirate operations, both in Dublin and in the rest of the country. ARD had just gone commercial with backing from Bernard Llewellyn, and again there had been no successful attempt to get that operation to close. Pirate radio stations were at this stage almost entitled to squatters' rights.

One of Dublin's more colourful pirate stations was The Skull and Cross Bones Radio System (SCBRS). It had been on the air a couple of months before being raided not by the Department, but by a rival station. On Sept. 24th 1977, the station was broken into and vandalised. A Radio Dublin sticker was left. Eamon Cooke denied any knowledge of the attack, but SCBRS never again made it back on-air.

Early in 1978, Downtown Radio Dublin came on the air; it broadcast on 225m. ARD was on 257 and the original Radio Dublin on 253. Not to be outdone, the Irish language organisation *Conradh na Gaeilge* announced on January 21st that it was to launch an Irish language pirate ; one had already existed out west in Saor Radio Connemara!

" New legislation is being considered by the Government to seek to plug the existing legal loopholes. This to my mind is, I fear, the beginning of the end ..."
from *Sound Alternative*
May / June 1978

Anatomy of a Raid

The Department of Posts and Telegraphs were in a dilemma. Pirate stations should not exist, yet they did, openly flouting whatever law there was. There were three ways the stations could be silenced:

a. The Law,
b. The Courts, and
c. Brute Force.

As explained, the hopelessly out of date 1926 Wireless Telegraphy Act could-n't cope with the pirates. New laws would have to be introduced to supplement or replace it. The Department however could do nothing about this, it was up to the politicians.

Through the courts? There was a problem. Some confusion existed about the previously explained loop-holes in the 1926 Act. What is more "the right of the citizens to express freely their convictions and opinions" is enshrined in the Constitution of the Republic. Judicial proceedings then could well backfire on the Department, with the pirates winning legitimacy on a legal technicality. The result then would be a carbon copy of what happened in Italy, with pirates being legalised through the courts. If the Italian parallel continued the next stop could well be pirate TV, with its endless diet of cheap quiz shows where the contestants usually end up with no clothes on - that would *never* do!

So the Department chose option number three: brute force, and that patently wasn't working.

It was time for a re-think.

The confusion that existed within the Department is made clear in a letter marked "Very Urgent" and dated 31st January 1978. In this letter the Department of Posts and Telegraphs seeks legal advice from two senior counsel, Mr. T.J. Connolly S.C., and Mr. J. McCarthy S.C. (The Department's file on the subject of pirate radio was included, as was a copy of the 1926 Act and the Broadcasting Authority Act, 1960):

"Counsel is requested to advise as a matter of urgency, whether it is unconstitutional for my Department to refuse to grant any pirate station a broadcasting licence and also to advise that if it should occur that one of these pirate stations commenced legal action, either seeking an injunction to prevent the Gardai or my Department interfering in any way with its broadcasting operations, or seeking a Court Order that the refusal to grant a licence was unconstitutional, would such a procedure effectively stop or prevent my Department from carrying out raids on other pirate stations, or from introducing new legislation to combat or outlaw pirate radio stations?"

Previous to this Mr. Callandar and his raiding parties had been trying to close stations by main force. But the raids on Radio Dublin only succeeded in lengthening not shortening broadcasting hours and putting the station on a commercial footing. In the months following the letter to Senior Counsel, the Department's raids grew fewer and fewer, only to resume with venom and vengeance in May. By then, it is safe to assume, Senior Counsel replied and the contents of the letters can be guessed at: that it was not unconstitutional to refuse broadcast licences or to raid the stations and that if a court case were to arise, the chances of it being won by the pirates were remote.

Mutiny for the Bounty!

By March of 1978 Radio Dublin, which still announced 'Radio Dublin, the Big D, on 253', had changed its postal address from the obscure 20 Ranelagh, to 3 Sarsfield Road, Eamon's home address. They also used his home phone number, 758684. Eamon Cooke had become public property. With people coming and going all day, with the constant fear of a raid and with a radio station broadcasting around the clock, Eamon was living on his nerves. So when one of the station's advertisers offered him a free week in Spain, he accepted, packed his bags and left the station, and his home, in the trust of his disc jockeys. His wife went to stay with her mother in Booterstown, and the Captain, DJ Sylvie and three others left for sunny Spain.

Station DJ James Dillon called together all of the Radio Dublin staff and in true revolutionary style he produced a manifesto to be signed. It stated (none too bluntly) that they were unhappy with Cooke's management and wished to leave Radio Dublin. Several disc jockeys, especially Neil O'Shea, had serious reservations about the strongly worded document. Nevertheless it was steamrolled through. That Monday the Radio Dublin schedule changed, and the station announced itself simply as The Big D. Radio Dublin was never mentioned. By Tuesday it was claimed that the Captain was no longer in charge of Radio Dublin, that he had sold out to big business. That day too Eamon Cooke was accused of being a child molestor. After his return from Spain, Cooke rightly pointed out that allegations like those "...are the type...which people cannot disprove, they can deny them, certainly, they can deny them like myself until I am blue in the face." By mid-week then, in the words of Declan Meehan "...it had really got into the nasties."

On Friday a tape recording was allegedly made. This recording was supposed to contain the evidence of Cooke's child molesting. Two female receptionists are meant to have been involved in the manufacture of the tape, under instructions from Frank Murray - the man Cooke had spoken so highly of after the Christmas '77 broadcasts. When the tape was completed, it is alleged that Gerry Campbell, a station DJ, brought it to the local priests at the Oblate Church, Inchicore. The tape, if it ever existed, has not surfaced since. But one thing is certain and that is that every effort was made during Cooke's absence to drag his name through the mud.

43

The Big D 'conspirators' were James Dillon, Mike Eastwood (Michael Cotter), John Paul (O'Brien), Gerry Campbell and Shay West (Seamus McLoughlin), the big name DJs in Radio Dublin. But every disc jockey had to make the choice, to leave for the Big D, or to stay. The choice was far from being an open one. DJs Neil O'Shea, Keiran Murray and Declan Meehan remember the promises that the conspirators made. In Declan's own words they "...promised them all sorts of programmes and everything," while Keiran Murray left "thinking I was going to get paid." With promises of this nature, it is not surprising that all of the Radio Dublin staff were swept along by the enthusiasm of the Big D ringleaders.

In the weeks prior to Cooke's departure the plans were laid. The new station was to have its studios in Chapel Lane, the new transmitter was ready to go into action. Up to this Cooke's station was still calling itself 'Radio Dublin, The Big D'. When he left, the station became 'The Big D' though still coming from Cooke's house on 253 metres, using the Radio Dublin transmitter. On the Sunday of Cooke's return, it was planned to vacate Inchicore and head to Chapel Lane.

As the Captain was enjoying his last morning of Spanish sunshine, at 10.25 am the Radio Dublin transmitter went on fire. Keiran Murray was on the air at the time, ironically playing the song 'We Love the Pirates' by the Roaring Sixties. He and some other disc jockeys ran upstairs to unplug the burning transmitter but there was "white, white, white smoke. The kind of smoke that was stinging your eyes, hurting your lungs, it was just very very bad. I remember there was just a mass of wires and valves and junk...it was so bad we had to run out again and close the door." Eventually Keiran battled his way through the acrid smoke and unplugged the transmitter, but the damage had been done. At the time Keiran told the press that four weeks non-stop broadcasting must have been "too much" for the transmitter, but today he is not too sure. It was some coincidence that it should go on fire the very day of Cooke's return, the very day the staff were leaving. Sabotage has never been proved, but it cannot be ruled out. James Dillon said that they "fully intended leaving the station in running order but without the manpower." Once the DJs were gone, Radio Dublin wouldn't be long in folding up.

That night Cooke returned home. He was met at the airport by James Dillon and Gerry Campbell. They briefed the Captain on the situation. James remembers that Eamon "...was a bit stunned, but he didn't show any signs of emotion. He claimed he didn't know how it could have happened" and that Big D "would collapse over night."

On the way home from the airport Eamon tuned up and down the dial, 253 was silent, only ARD were broadcasting "and they sounded very happy," the Captain commented at the time. On returning home Cooke found "..practically nothing there, no transmitter, nothing worked, no tapes...and all the staff were gone as well."

The condition of Cooke's house and its contents is still a subject of controversy. The transmitter was burnt out, and the place did reek of smoke as every window in the place was sealed and barricaded, but whether records were broken or stickers were burned, messing did take place. James Dillon denies any organised attempt to vandalise Cooke's home, "...the place was always overrun with kids, there could be ten or fifteen kids answering the phone. I think probably they had something to do with some of the messing that went on." Damage was done, but as Declan Meehan observed "I'm sure Cooke exaggerated it."

Monday, the day following his return, Eamon was broadcasting again but there was "fairly hopeless reception". During the week his transmitting range extended and the following Sunday the Captain went on air at 1.32pm to explain his side of the story. His explanation took the best part of two hours.

The roots of the Radio Dublin staff mutiny go back to late 1977. Prior to Christmas of that year money had begun to flow into the station, but disc jockeys and other staff saw very little of it. Although in the week following the mutiny, James Dillon, Mike Eastwood and Gerry Campbell, denied that money had anything to do with the split, to entirely dismiss financial motives would be hasty. A lot of money was floating around the pirate radio world, and doubtless the three DJs mentioned would have liked a larger share than they were getting. Keiran Murray remembers that although none of the Big D disc jockeys were paid "I saw Gerry Campbell and the like getting a wad of notes into their hand because himself and James Dillon and Noel Kirwin were all partners, so any money that came in went to them." Although financial considerations may not have been the prime reason for the split, they were certainly an important secondary reason.

Initially it was James Dillon's idea to set up another radio station. His reasons for leaving Radio Dublin were that, "At the time of the split, there were certain things in the station and with Eamon Cooke that I wasn't happy with, and for a number of reasons I decided to leave the station...I didn't like the way Eamon Cooke personally handled himself and some of the circumstances arising in the station I found just unacceptable. Now some of the other guys afterwards claimed that they left because they felt the station had gone stale and other people said they left for money reasons and other people left because they saw it as a sinking ship."

The reasons for the split were many and varied, and Eamon Cooke's own eccentric personality certainly didn't help matters. So when the Captain left the country and Dillon's plans for a professional, commercial radio station were released, the mass exodus of staff was understandable.

Dillon, at first, wanted to site his station in Cork, but "we were advised it was a closed shop." So he decided to set up his station in Dublin. In the weeks prior to Cooke's departure, the plans for what was to become The Big D were finalised. The studios were to be in Chapel Lane, and financial backing was to come from Noel Kirwin, an advertiser with Radio Dublin and owner of a small chain of boutiques. With everything ready to roll the only factor left was the timing of the split. Dillon is emphatic that "...it wasn't really an orchestrated thing, to get him (Cooke) away and then do the split." It may not have been orchestrated, but having Cooke out of the country was exactly what Dillon needed, it would from his point of view make the break a lot cleaner and easier.

Cooke's holiday had been supplied free of charge by 'Jet Sun Travel', advertisers with Radio Dublin. Although the holiday was arranged through Frank Murray, one of the ringleaders, it is doubtful that the holiday was planned with the sole purpose of overthrowing 'The Captain'. However it is no coincidence that The Big D was set up the week that Cooke left the country. What is a coincidence is that the holiday arrangements and the plans to set up The Big D all happened at more or less the same time. Initially The Big D transmitter, home-made by Radio Dublin engineer John Kane, was due for completion "...three weeks before Eamon Cooke went on holidays," but when the holiday plans became known to the conspirators, they wasted no time in turning it to their advantage. Their plans were totally successful, but they failed to consider one factor: Eamon Cooke's stubborn personality. James Dillon never expected Radio Dublin would make it back, "...the best part of Radio Dublin was the staff," he observed. Now they had left, and only the unpredictable Cooke had survived.

During the week of his return, Cooke advertised that on Sunday's Station News he would explain his part of the story. Dillon remembers "...some people started running scared, some of them left town before he got home.." To understand their attitude towards Cooke, we must know the man. Only then can we appreciate why so many people ran so far.

The Captain.....

Eamon Cooke was born on November 4th 1936, in Derravaragh Road, Kimmage. While still young his parents moved to Phibsboro where Eamon went to St. Vincent's Christian Brothers. Cooke describes his parents as "Ultra-Republican", and some of their ideology certainly rubbed off on their son Eamon. After flitting from job to job, he was arrested by the Gardai for Republican activities and in Cooke's own words, "I certainly had to spend some time in Portlaoise and the Curragh". After his release he got involved in electronics and went into business with an electrical shop in Thomas Street. Before getting involved in radio, Cooke had risen to fame in the pages of the *Sunday World* for his vigilante activities. Eamon would tune in to the police frequencies and when an emergency or disturbance was reported, he would jump into his Jaguar and speed off up the back streets to help the police apprehend the criminals!

The exact date the Captain became involved in radio is a movable feast, either 1966 or 1973 or as late as 1976 or 1977 - depending on who he's talking to.

But the date is of little consequence. By the time Cooke took over from a reluctant Dr. Don, he was already a well-known eccentric. His republican views, his manner, his habit of wearing worn out clothes and speaking as if from a pulpit on Sunday's 'Station News', all gave him an image that was to stick. For the DJs the most frightening thing about the Captain was his personality. While in prison he studied psychology and prided himself on his supposed ability to judge a person's character or personality at a glance: all very disturbing should you get on the wrong side of him. His eccentricity and connections with the Republican movement meant that his reaction to the staff mutiny could not be guessed. He might do anything.

The week of his return from Spain, Cooke came on the air every day promoting his 'Station News' for the following Sunday. This was to be his revenge. Doubtless all the renegade disc jockeys were tuned in to 253 metres, at 1.32 pm that Sunday April 16th 1978, for Eamon Cooke's now infamous testament as Ken Sheehan has dubbed it.

....And his Testament

Cooke's sermon from the mount lasted nearly two hours. He explained, "I'm trying in this news to stick to bare, basic facts," so sounding like a reasonable man he continued, never stating any untruths, just implying them, and never making any threats. He was much more subtle. The Captain can do amazing things with a single turn of phrase, and if you are on the bad side of him, a lot can be read into his vague suggestions. "If I don't mention some things, and name out names, that's because I just simply have not absolute proof of them." No-one could guess what he knew. For example, "My wife (his second), is I'm sure, inside listening away to the radio there, wondering why I must dig up so much, well it's already been dug up for me, as one of our ex-staff , Miss Kathryn O'Kelly said, 'we all have our little secrets.' Yes, we all have our little secrets, everyone out there has some little secret he wants to hide away." Kathryn O'Kelly's "little secret" was her marriage to Big D ringleader James Dillon. As for all the other little secrets? No one slept soundly for a long time.

During the news, Cooke sounded so reasonable and understanding. He mentioned every criticism that had been levelled against him, and explained it away logically. Cooke even gave listeners permission to listen to The Big D if they so wished, but qualified that statement with the beautiful, "It is unfortunate - as I've told many of the staff since - a broadcasting licence would have been theirs within about eight weeks. Eight short weeks! They would have been able to hold up their heads and wear a Radio Dublin badge around town and be congratulated, sign autographs and everything, and what is the situation now?"

Cooke explained how he found his belongings scattered, his furniture broken and his personal papers rifled and read. How DJ Sylvie worked undercover for him at The Big D, and how she collapsed from exhaustion that Tuesday. How Frank Murray was "the only man whom I would like to see really taken down a peg," and how Cooke had held out against a £250,000 offer for a 60% share in Radio Dublin! Yes indeed, the Captain was a great man for the fisherman's tale.

The Big D

The Big D officially began broadcasting from Chapel Lane at 5am in the early hours of Monday April 10th 1978. Transmissions ceased at 10.15am. The next day the station began 24 hour a day broadcasting. Dillon remembers there was a great sense of excitement and a "fabulous atmosphere" at Big D up to Christmas. "We were becoming celebrities," grinned Declan Meehan, "and that was completely new to us!" After the station was set up, many DJs left ARD and joined up with The Big D in Chapel Lane.

While Dillon described relations between the Dublin stations as "healthy rivalry" others felt the atmosphere was a little unhealthy. Eamon Cooke would accuse ARD of cutting his aerial, they would accuse him of sending live spiders through the post, while gangs armed with batons and bottles were ready to defend the Radio Dublin transmitter against any interference from ARD or The Big D.

Barely three months after opening, on June 15th, The Big D was raided and over £7,000 worth of equipment including the transmitter was taken. DJ Dennis Murray remembers, "Fifteen gardai, who had removed their numbers, smashed their way into the Big D. They were accompanied by plain clothes detectives who just ripped everything out, smashed the place up and generally enjoyed themselves."

However, with the help of "a secret backer" the station got back on the air. That backer was Dillon's 22 year old partner Noel Kirwin, but the alias sounded better to the press. And there was plenty of coverage as the Big D transmitter was hauled away, and even more when the Courts ruled that the equipment should be returned. Slowly, raids by the Department became less frequent until eventually they went into hibernation. "We were getting too much good publicity out of it," said Cooke, and that is one of the main reasons the raids ceased.

Although there were two factions within The Big D, there were "no rows". But still, there was the ex-Radio Dublin crew and the crew from ARD, both with different views on broadcasting - James Dillon described the situation as a "healthy conflict". The ex-ARD team drew up their own schedule and presented it to Dillon. Declan Meehan described it as "something experimental - like London Weekend Television... " And so Big D Weekend radio was born and Davitt Kelly was in charge. The station operated from Friday until 3am Monday morning, and boasted an impressive line-up of DJs including John Clarke, Mark Storey, Gerry Ryan, Marty Whelan, Dave Heffernan, P.J. Curtis,

The aftermath of the raid of June 15th. Dennis Murray is holding the record, behind him is Tony Dixon, and on the right is Ross Talon.

Declan Meehan and Neil O'Shea. In Declan's own words "when you look at the line-up, Jesus you know, these are all the best guys!" Although Big D weekend was experimental, James Dillon admits "it ran very, very well," and although weekend advertising never amounted to a substantial sum, the programming was tight and public reaction was favourable.

Big D and Big D Weekend continued throughout 1978, and those days were the most successful the two stations ever had. During the week the 'in' personalities hosted the shows, names like Gerry Campbell, Dave John, James Dillon, John Paul, Marty Hall, Tony Dixon and Dave Fanning all made The Big D a big success. These DJs were mostly defectors from Radio Dublin, while Big D Weekend mainly contained ex-ARD staff, who, led by Davitt Kelly, were ultimately to seek more elbow room.

Advert placed by Big D in 'In Dublin' shortly after the fire in Chapel Lane

Towards the end of 1978, Davitt Kelly called together a group of Big D disc-jockeys. His plan was to set up a new radio station and to extend the Big D Weekend format over a whole week. Word of this meeting got back to James Dillon who gave Davitt his walking papers. Dillon remembers that Davitt "was responsible, not only for the staff, but the premises, he was given full responsibility for the Weekend. I thought, to use his position to call the staff together.... and to use it as a recruiting ground for the new station, I thought wasn't on." This is rather ironic considering this is exactly what Dillon and Co. did to Eamon Cooke of Radio Dublin. When Davitt left The Big D, Declan Meehan and Robbie Irwin did too, but Mark Storey stayed. Though only the three left "effectively the Weekend concept fell down." It was the first of many disasters to strike The Big D.

On Thursday November 30th 1978, Noel Kirwin, co-owner of The Big D, stormed out. He had had an argument with staff members over telephone costs. Frustrated and annoyed he sped away from the Chapel Lane studios. Later that day he was involved in a car crash at the Merrion Gates. He was rushed to St. Vincent's Hospital but subsequently died. It was a terrible blow, and all the staff at The Big D were reported to be "stunned". James Dillon would now have to pick up the pieces and carry on alone.

Although Bernard Llewellyn did much to bring pirate radio out of the back room and into the open, still only ARD had anything resembling a studio. Even then a reporter of the day wasn't very impressed with things at Belvedere Place: "The studio looked rather bleak," he wrote, "its walls covered with shiny tin-foil reflecting the glare from the single light bulb on the roof"! At Radio Dublin, they kept to the fine traditions of hobby stations right to the very end. Disco decks would be balanced precariously on table tops, records and cassettes would be strewn all over the place, ashtrays would overflow onto tape machines and wires criss-crossed the floor, like so much spaghetti.

When the Captain opened Radio Dublin Channel 2, it occupied the room across the hall from Radio Dublin proper. The kitchen (at the far end of the hall) was always crammed with people, some coming in, others going out and more just standing around. Cooke also hoarded things - broken record decks, bits of radio sets, wire, even fuses. All these trophies were stacked to overflowing in a small room off the kitchen. Whenever he needed anything, in he'd go, wire cutters in hand, only to emerge moments later, dusty but triumphant!

Although The Big D sounded professional, in reality the studios in Chapel Lane were little better than those of Radio Dublin. The station was based in an old closed up factory with a hole in the roof. The station was always cold and damp, and electric fires were constantly burning away. In the very early, freezing hours of Tuesday 2nd January 1979 there were just three people left at The Big D. Dave Fanning, who had just finished his show, John Paul who was to take over, and James Dillon. Fanning had come off air at 3am, but was unable to get a taxi home, so Dillon offered him a lift, which Dave accepted. Before starting they decided to warm up in a local late night coffee shop, John Paul joined them, and a taped programme was put on air.

When they returned, The Big D was in flames.

It had been barely five weeks since the tragic death of Noel Kirwin, and now the station was gutted. However The Big D returned to the air within days, ironically using equipment that had been returned by the Department of Posts and Telegraphs following that last highly publicised raid of June 15th.

While The Big D was dogged with problems in late '78 and '79, ARD was enjoying a fairly stable existence. Although advertising revenue was relatively low, ARD still managed to keep their programming highly professional. After Davitt Kelly was evicted from The Big D, Declan Meehan and Robbie Irwin rejoined ARD. Declan remembers Bernard Llewellyn speaking of ARD as "the new station, the one they will write books about."

In December news broke that was to rock the pirate radio world. RTE were to launch a second national radio station - a popular music channel, Radio 2.

5

A
Radio
Jungle

*"Pirate radio stations are still bursting out
like acne all over the adolescent airwaves."*
Irish Times, 19th April 1983.

Apart from the fantasies of power and wealth,
there was no overall 'grand design' to any of the
stations popping up all over the country.
Rumours of vast profits had encouraged publi-
cans, restaurateurs and shopkeepers to turn out-
houses, broom closets and lofts into radio stations. Most of these ventures folded soon

after opening, while others carried on using volunteers and secondhand compilation albums. In reality profits were there, but before milking the market it had to be captured. This would involve the investment of sizeable amounts in records and equipment, something Ireland's budding media moguls were unwilling to do. Everyone was paddling, as yet no one dreamed of diving off at the deep end.

Between March and August 1978, the number of pirates operating around the country exploded from a handful to around twenty five. There were ten in the capital, three in each of the cities Cork, Limerick, and Galway and about six more scattered around the country. Setting up a station was easy. Take for example Radio Carousel in Dundalk.

In May 1978 Hugh Hardy called to The Big D to recruit disc jockeys. John Kane, the Big D engineer, had already built him a transmitter. DJs Eric Vaughan, John Paul and Keiran Murray decided to join this new station, which didn't even have a name. Keiran Murray remembers, "I looked up at the record library in The Big D and the first record I saw was K-Tel's 'Carousel' and I said to Hugh Hardy, 'What about calling it Carousel, look you even have a theme tune there, Don't stop the Carousel.' He said, 'right, OK!'" So with the album tucked under his arm Hugh led the company to partner Phil Monaghan's Dundalk Shopping Centre, home of Radio Carousel. The station was just a room "full of rubbish", but Hugh borrowed the phone line from the manager's office, and the top twenty from a local record shop. Keiran recalls "I just said, 'welcome to Radio Carousel, 265 metres, our phone line here is 024 - ', whatever it was. The instant I announced it, the phone rang...it rang and rang and rang and never stopped ringing." On July 7th Carousel was raided, but was back on the air in no time. The station had become a runaway success, so much so that Hardy built up his own carousel of four radio stations around the country. One of these was Radio Carousel Navan, and Hardy put Murray in charge of setting it up in October 1981.

Keiran recalls that setting up a radio station had become easier than ever. The one hundred and ten foot mast was the most expensive item, at around £2,000. "A set of record decks would cost about £150 to £200. A mixer probably about £500." As for the total cost of setting up a station "I'd say about £2,500 roughly, maybe £3,000. But I know he'd made his money within a couple of months."

The hardware then was relatively cheap; radio only became expensive when content and presentation came into consideration. Professionalism is expensive. Stations which were unashamedly commercial did have a sizeable outlay. Any sum from a couple of thousand to a couple of hundred thousand pounds would be tied up in equipment that could at any moment be seized by the Department. The stakes then were high, but so potentially were the rewards.

The pirates as a whole were slow in realising the latent profitability of radio. Most were happy getting a small but secure return on an equally small investment. Even at the height of its glory in 1978, The Big D only charged £100 for a half hour sponsored programme. Commercial radio in Ireland was completely underexploited.

By the late seventies pirate radio in Ireland had got into a rut. Stations had expanded and developed as far as they could. While the on-air talent did exist, the business acumen needed to tap the crock of gold did not. A whole new approach was needed. The next stage in the development of Irish radio would require not only massive injections of capital, but also management, marketing and professional skills, than possessed only by foreigners, people who had experience of real commercial radio, who were used to threats from impotent government, and who knew how to make a station sound professional.

Mark Storey summed up the situation in a letter to *In Dublin* magazine in February 1978. He said that people listened to pirate stations like Radio Dublin and ARD not "because RTE is a bad service, they are listened to because RTE is inadequate - the old problem of pleasing all of the people all of the time, as well as saving the language and the faith and getting off the air before midnight to keep in with the unions."

It hadn't taken much to woo listeners away from RTE, and it would take even less to woo them away from the existing pirates.

Around the Country

RTE has been operating local radio in Cork since 1974. By 1978 'Corkabout' broadcast for one hour, five days a week. This meagre service was the sum total of RTE's regular de-centralised broadcasting until the advent of the Irish language station, Radio na Gaeltachta. It didn't satisfy listeners and soon Cork City was a hive of pirate activity.

One of Cork's initial pirate stations was the Cork Broadcasting Company (CBC). The two men behind the operation were DJ Daniel (Don Walsh), and Stevie Bolger, who was later to work for RTE in the country's second city. About a week before the staff mutiny at Radio Dublin on March 21st, the CBC was raided. By July Stevie Bolger had grown unhappy with the programme output and left to set up Alternative Broadcasting Cork (ABC) with his partner Tony Gannon. CBC programming differed from that of ABC. In fact the former station was more in line with the non-stop music format of Radio Dublin and ARD, while ABC, Stevie's new station, had more community involvement, news and interviews. ABC's broadcasting hours were also longer, lasting 20 hours a day during the week and around the clock at weekends.

However ambitious Stevie's station was, the radio critic of the *Irish Times* was not impressed. Mary Leland complained about Cork disc jockeys "...who cannot even speak English properly - who cannot, it seems, even read the headlines from the *Cork Examiner* without obvious verbal anxiety and difficulty." The Department must have agreed with her because on September 13th both

CBC and ABC were raided. As with their Dublin counterparts the stations cobbled together a transmitter and were back on the air within twenty four hours.

The month of May proved to be a very active time for pirate radio in Dundalk. Early that month Radio Dundalk came on stream, operated by three local DJs. The station wasn't running long before being raided on May 7th. Although the transmitter was seized Radio Dundalk was back on the air within hours, only to be raided again on July 13th. After an all-night session with a soldering iron, the station returned the following day.

During the active year of 1978, other stations to pop up around the country included Radio Tralee Community. The finance for this station came from local publican Danny Leane, and the presenters included Michael Dwyer, who had a weekly film review spot. Michael also reviewed films on The Big D.

Out West and Independent Radio Galway (IRG) came in the wake of RTE's community radio experiment in the area. Finance for the station came from local TV rental entrepreneur Tom O'Connor. IRG operated from 11am to 6pm and had a low-power transmitter. On June 26th IRG was raided and it was claimed that around £1,000 of equipment was taken. At the time a spokesman for the station said that they operated on a "shoestring budget", but this didn't stop them getting back on the air within days.

In the Southeast, Waterford's first pirate station, Waterford Local Radio (WLR), started regular broadcasting on June 25th, from "a number of locations", as one of the backers put it. By late 1978 Limerick City was buzzing with pirate activity. The city boasted no less than four stations. Capital Radio Limerick was one of the early ones. It was raided on July 29th, and three months later in October CRL announced that it was to close. A statement was released: "In the light of recent government decisions on the matter, we feel that it would be advisable at this stage to cease our illegal operations in the hope that more serious consideration would be given by the authorities to our application for a broadcasting licence."

It was to be the first of many stations to cease operations in a vain attempt to impress unimpressable governments and to show that they favoured the spirit of broadcasting and not its commercialism. Whether they were sincere or not we will never know.

The city's second station was Radio Limerick Weekly Echo (RLWE). This station was unique in that it was controlled by the local newspaper, the *Limerick Weekly Echo*, much to the disgust of the leader writers in the city's other weekly, the *Limerick Leader*. RLWE was operated by John Marrnett and Dick Sadlier and the station gave generous advertising to its mother newspaper. On August 9th RLWE was raided. Station manager John Frawley announced that WLER would return, with bigger and better equipment. Late 1978 also saw English DJ Mike Richardson setting up The Big L. While initially slow to take off, the professional Big L eventually swamped the other local stations; for example,

Independent Radio Limerick, a hobby station with very irregular broadcasting hours, faded as time passed.

October 1978, saw the launch of Radio Midlands from Athlone and within weeks Westmeath had a second pirate station, Big M on 217 metres, operating from Mullingar.

Green and Red Lights

All this pirate activity was preceded by several events early in 1978. Towards the end of June Minister for Posts and Telegraphs Faulkner moved an estimate of £150 million for his Department. This sparked off questions from the opposition parties on the subject of pirate radio. Tom O'Donnell, Fianna Fail spokesman on Transport and Communications wanted to know what the Minister proposed to do about the radio pirates and Labour's John Horgan added that the Minister's lack of action was lowering morale in RTE. Mr. Faulkner replied with the predictable ministerial cliché that draft legislation was being prepared and would be introduced in the next Dail session.

This lack of direction from the Government, coupled with the failure of the Department's raids, plus the lure of advertising, gave the go-ahead to pirates all over the country. Although legislation had been promised on numerous occasions there was still no sign of it being introduced. On the subject of pirate radio, Fianna Fail TD Michael Keating felt that "law breaking is relative"; not only that but Dublin County Council passed a motion calling for the licensing of Radio Dublin and ARD. Whatever the future held in store, for the present pirate radio was degenerating into an unregulated free for all. If licences were on the horizon however, a lot of money could be made. Therefore the time to act was now, so John E. Nolan set up the Eire Broadcasting Corporation (EBC).

On 22nd June 1978 Capital Radio Dublin was raided, which resulted in Mr. Alan Russell from the station and some DJs picketing the Dail.

In October the PMPA succeeded in getting an injunction against East Coast Radio, who were operating from Unit 5, Chatham House, Chatham Street. The PMPA claimed that the station could be heard over the telephones. After this, East Coast moved to Crumlin and soon afterwards stopped broadcasting altogether.

In June 1978, John E. Nolan, signing himself "director of the EBC", circulated a proposal on local radio to those who might be interested in financing stations. In an open letter to Dublin County Council after they had passed the above mentioned motion, John E. Nolan stated: "You have correctly identified the grassroots demand for local radio..." However, Nolan did not want to see the existing pirates get a licence, rather he preferred an open franchise system, whereby his EBC would control local radio. After announcing his willingness to partake in local radio, John E. Nolan retired to prepare a draft proposal on the subject.

The EBC wasn't the only organisation ready to scramble for licences. Michael Tiernan, an ex-ARD advertising representative, set up the National Independent Broadcasting Organisation (NIBO) as an umbrella group to cover some pirates concerns. The aims of the NIBO were to raise the standard of member stations and to squeeze out smaller pirate operations. By September 1979 the NIBO claimed 100% support from ARD, Carousel, IRG, WLR and ABC, Cork. Michael planned to police members by monitoring the output of stations and by using only unionised staff. Also the best programmes from each station would be made available to the others in the NIBO, and through a network system, nationwide local advertising could be offered to companies. But as Eamon Cooke observed, "the idea was good, but it doesn't really work." Neither did Michael Tiernan's plan to bring Minister Faulkner to the European Court. It seemed that in 1978 stations were still unwilling to co-operate.

Meanwhile, Young Fine Gael released a document sympathising with the pirates, and not to be outdone, outspoken Senator John A. Murphy replied to it, "On an entirely inadequate survey basis, Young Fine Gael has called for the legalisation of commercial radio, this following the lead given by Deputy John Kelly some time ago. It is lamentable that responsible politicians should thus lend themselves to the squalid purposes of ruthless and anonymous commercial exploiters. The Young Fine Gael discussion document correctly points out that the law is presently being flouted but erroneously deduces that the remedy is to make the law yield to the same powerful pressures that hitherto have shown such contempt for the public interest...The sole business of the pirate radios is to make money...If the pirates are legalised, the national broadcasting service will be under pressure to lower its standards and the 'choice' will tend increasingly to be between non-stop pop and non-stop pop."

Strong words indeed, but it wasn't to end there. The above mentioned John Kelly, Fine Gael spokesman on Industry, Commerce and Energy, drafted a reply. He accepted that commercial radio tends towards the lowest common denominator, "but he is on very thin ice," Kelly said of the Senator, "if he implies that a particular medium of communication should be reserved for those who pass an officially-prescribed test of culturally uplifting content."

Never ones to slack, Young Fine Gael also replied to Senator Murphy saying that "local radio....would not, contrary to Senator Murphy's expectations, provide a non-stop diet of pop music, rather it would contribute greatly to the quality of life in the vicinity." The Young Fine Gael group had confused 'Community' radio with 'Commercial' radio, probably not deliberately, but through a naivety that typified years of political inactivity on the subject of unlicensed radio.

Commercial v Community Radio

The first hot-air blows had been struck in an argument that was to drag on for years. The Fine Gael reply to Senator Murphy summed up a lot of the confusion that existed and still exists on the subject of community access broadcasting.

Licensing the pirates would have solved one problem in that they would no longer be illegal, but would have led to another, the same problem that cropped up in the UK nearly twenty years after the banning of the off-shore pirates. In this case those denied access to the airwaves set up their own ethnic stations, playing for the most part to an audience not being catered for by Independent Radio or the BBC. By early 1988 there were around thirty two landbased pirate stations operating in London, and easily twice that number around the remainder of the UK.

On March 30th 1979, the Taoiseach Jack Lynch made an announcement at the Jacobs Radio and Television Awards. In front of a crowd that consisted of mainly RTE personnel and advertising agencies, he outlined new plans to establish legitimate local radio and ban the pirates. Shortly after this shock announcement, on April 10th, the Wireless Telegraphy Bill 1979 was circulated. The Bill intended to wipe out the pirates. Fines of £10,000 or 2 years in prison could be imposed on disc jockeys, advertisers and station directors. It would become an offence to participate in programmes or even to supply a station with records.

In an atmosphere of speculation and rumour, yet another attempt was made to unify the pirates and so present a coherent case for legitimacy. This time ARD took the initiative and tried to organise a merger with Big D and Radio Dublin. Again pride stood in the way of co-operation and the idea never became a reality. It looked as if the pirates were about to walk the plank. The promised Independent Local Radio Authority
was planned for later in the year, as was RTE's
new pop radio channel, Radio 2.

Comin'atcha!

In 1976 RTE presented a "comprehensive plan for radio" to the government of the day. Contained in this were plans to extend the

The first record played on Radio 2 was "Clockwork" by the Boomtown Rats.

broadcasting monopoly by introducing a second national radio channel and local radio in main urban areas.

Contrary to popular belief, RTE does not control its own destiny. Permission must be got from the Minister for Posts and Telegraphs (now the Minister of Communications) for an extension of broadcasting hours or the introduction of opt-out programmes. Decisions then lie with the Minister and not with the RTE Authority. Therefore, if the national broadcasting organisation wishes to extend its service, or to introduce a new channel or even a new transmitter, permission must be granted by the Minister in consultation with the sitting government.

When RTE decided to set up local radio and a second radio station in 1976, the Minister had to be informed and he had to give the project the go-ahead, "We always expected that the local radio plan would come first," said Billy Wall, the first head of Radio 2, "because that was the priority we were giving it, the priority we felt was necessary and we were very surprised when in 1978 we were given the go-ahead not for the local radio aspect of the plan, but for the second national radio channel to be aimed at young people." So RTE was given the green light for Radio 2, but permission to operate a local radio service was withheld.

In December 1978, Billy Wall, who at the time was a light entertainment producer in Radio Eireann, was appointed head of the new station. The date for getting Radio 2 on the air was set at May 31st, a short five months away. Billy recalls that "it was good that we had the thirty-first of May. It wasn't going to change, therefore all the arrangements for the new station had to be made in a very short time." The last day in May wasn't just any arbitrary date. It was chosen because it was the day on which the old RTE Authority were to stand down, and they wanted the new station to arrive during their term of office!

Before the advent of Radio 2, RTE's pop music output was restricted to Pat Kenny's 'Nightbus' programme, the odd slot from Ken Stewart, the one hour top twenty with Jimmy Greely and Larry Gogan's programme (on FM) during the afternoons. Billy Wall remembers that these programmes, "were taking account of the need." A need that Radio 2 would attempt to satisfy.

The station did make it on the air by the end of May. There had been uncharacteristically few problems with the unions. Disc jockeys would for the first time operate their own record decks, and the new manning levels meant that only six full-time and two part-time producers were necessary. But the station also needed presenters. The search was on, a search which Declan Meehan labelled the 'Panic Job'. "Everyone was ringing up for an audition," he recalled, " sort of, 'Hello there, I do an hour on Radio City and I want to do an audition.' 'Oh Yes sir!, come in next Monday night and bring four records!'" There was a marked similarity between the first Radio 2 schedule and that of ARD and The Big D: "...that's how they decided the schedule - where are they on the pirates?" was Declan Meehan's comment. James Dillon also agreed that the similarity was more than a coincidence, in a station that employed mostly ex-pirates.

RTE's Michael Carroll described the speed with which Radio 2 was set up as "a miracle", but there were several things left undone. The negotiations for the Radio 2 news service were not completed by 31st May 1979 and the station had to wait over four years for that. When the news finally did arrive, it was off the air within a day due to union pressure, only to reappear again on 27th August 1983. Teething problems aside the first audience survey published showed that Radio 2 had captured 56% of the 15 - 20 year old market, a figure Billy Wall was "highly satisfied with". In RTE's 1982 Annual Report, a profile is given of the new station; "As well as broadcasting Irish and International pop music, Radio 2 carries public service information and advice on its daytime programmes. Current Affairs and Cultural items are also featured, in addition to a wide range of music - traditional and folk music, rock, country and jazz - all aimed at the under twenty five listener."

As the battle for the ears of those under 25 (half the population of the Republic) began to hot up, many of Radio 2's "public service information" slots began to disappear. By late 1984 country, jazz and other minority music shows had either been axed or banished to Radio 1's off-peak programming wilderness where they were barely tolerated. By June 1985, a new schedule and a new boss, Cathal McCabe, finally relegated the last remnants of public service broadcasting to the closet.

End of a two-year reign - a farewell photo of the ARD crew

In the wake of the successful launch of Radio 2, Bernard Llewellyn claimed that while initially some advertising revenue had been lost, the pirates had quickly recovered, an assertion Billy Wall rejected. Either way by August, ARD was boasting of ad contracts worth £1,500 a week. Bernard's idea was to get ahead and stay ahead of Radio 2. He arranged for his star DJs like Steve Rhodes, DJ Sylvie and Paul Vincent to attend a crash course in radio presentation in Bay City Studios with Brian McKenzie and Tony Allan. Professionalism was the one thing Bernard Llewellyn strove for and invested heavily in. He had employed NUJ staff, which cost, and in the end contributed in no small way to the bankruptcy of his chain of TV shops - 'Anya TV'.

The summer of 1979 saw Llewellyn widening his base of operations and purchasing the Dublin freesheet *Northside*. Then in October he made a shock announcement: ARD was to close. "We are going off the air, to facilitate our application for a licence, and to that end we have already set up a consortium to prepare a submission." The station was to go off the air on New Year's Eve. However a co-operative of disc jockeys were to buy ARD's equipment and open a new station, Radio 257, in the Crofton Airport Hotel.

At the time legislation on local radio seemed inevitable, and whatever Llewellyn's real motives were for pulling out of broadcasting, Paul Vincent remembers that Bernard "thought he had done enough, he felt that licences were going to be issued soon." If Bernard and his consortium were waiting for a licence it would be a long wait.

257

The group of disc jockeys who bought out Bernard included Dave C., Ian Dempsey, Davitt Kelly and Paul Vincent. Paul recalls "one of the stipulations was that Dr. Don was not to have any part of Radio 257." In the end only Dave C. and Paul Vincent signed the takeover papers. This cost them £2,000 without the transmitter. They were now in control of Radio 257.

Paul Vincent was at the time, in his own words "a nice guy" and in his innocence he thought it would be a good idea if Dr. Don were a director "even though Bernard said that he shouldn't be. So we invited Dr. Don to get up his third of the money to buy ARD." Which he did. As Llewellyn was washing his hands of ARD, another Dublin station came on the air: Radio City broadcast on 260 metres near Radio Moscow, and so experienced a lot of nighttime interference. Therefore when ARD announced it was to close, Radio City decided to take over the 257 slot.

After a very emotional close-down, ARD kept the transmitter on broadcasting a heterodyne (high pitched tone), thus preventing Radio City from taking over the 257 frequency. Around midday on New Year's Day the ARD equipment was to be moved as planned from Belvedere Place to the Crofton Hotel. "What we were to do was to leave the station transmitter on with a heterodyne, while we went up with the big transmitter and plugged that in," said Paul Vincent. But unfortunately before the big transmitter got to the Crofton, the plug was pulled on the first transmitter in Belvedere Place. The heterodyne went off and Radio City moved in. Paul Vincent remembers that Paul Cotter, the City engineer, "had been sitting up all night for this to happen". It was not a good start to the year, and it was to get worse. At three that afternoon the 257 aerial at the Crofton was cut down. A crew from City were blamed and relations between the two stations got off on the wrong foot. Radio City continued broadcasting until early 1983, when the studios went on fire. Altogether the role it played in the development of Irish pirate radio is less than minimal.

Radio 257 (broadcasting on 259 metres), went from strength to strength. The initial line up was impressive and included: Steve Rhodes, Ian Dempsey, Paul Vincent, Dave C. and Jason Maine. Despite competition from Radio 2, the station proved very popular for a while. What finally pushed it to the wall was the arrival in Dublin of two ex-Caroline disc jockeys, Robbie Robinson and Chris Cary. These men were to change dramatically the face of Irish broadcasting.

All over the country stations were having to get used to living with Radio 2. For those at ARD and Big D it was hardest as the cream of their staff had joined RTE. James Dillon was glad to see the station DJs do so well, "we still had enough good disc jockeys to continue at the same level of broadcasting but a lot of the guys who continued on the air had applied to RTE and didn't get in, so there was a feeling that they were lesser DJs in a way...people's egos were deflated and one or two people left radio altogether." But this was not the complete reason for the 'downhill slope' that ARD and Big D found themselves on after the advent of Radio 2. James Dillon is convinced that both stations began to lose listeners because they lost direction. "The legislators had said that they intended having the stations closed down by Christmas...with comments like that, it doesn't really generate a lot of enthusiasm...In the first year, we saw it as a twelve month project, with the result that we got the work done. We had a Big D beach buggy, we'd a hundred thousand badges. The second year it was 'will we get Christmas out of it?'" With nothing to look forward to, and with a rumour of British capital coming to back a superpirate , the former giants of the radio world "weren't planning anything - we were just planning closing."

The Best Laid Plans

Two of the more interesting articles concerning local radio submitted to the government in 1979 came from John E. Nolan's EBC and from RTE. One deserves more consideration than the other, but in the end both were largely ignored.

John E. Nolan, brother of RTE's Liam Nolan, is best known for his commercial activities, in that he can provide a ready-made company off the shelf for a customer in less than ten minutes. Therefore it is doubtful if he had any problems setting up his Eire Broadcasting Corporation (EBC).

The EBC submission begins with an attempt to influence politicians. Each Ministerial post is mentioned with some of the advantages of Mr. Nolan's Independent Local Radio (ILR), listed alongside. For example:

Minister for Environment: Effective new medium for anti-litter and conservation campaigns.

Minister for Social Welfare: Less unemployed = less dole = more funds for welfare.

Minister for Posts and Telegraphs: Additional power to his department.

And there is more: "... all TDs would benefit... they might be able to lighten their workload by direct communication with constituents" and, "cannot fail but to reap the benefit in votes, when the next election comes around." This makes one wonder whether Nolan's ILR was meant for the people, or as a tool of political propaganda, and a platform for ego-tripping TDs. One final extract from this historic document will complete the farce:

Minister for Agriculture: New prompt medium for harvesting, sowing and for agricultural campaigns.

That final argument for Nolan's vision of Independent Local Radio is, more or less, the same as that used in favour of state controlled broadcasting back in 1923! If RTE had failed to reach the farming community, commercial radio, with "65% music content", would have no hope. Eamon Cooke summed up John E. Nolan in saying, "I won't say anything bad...but the man was in it just for the money."

The RTE document on local radio is much more down to earth, and was passed by the Authority on 14th December 1979. It points out that should local radio be given over to private enterprise, RTE's revenue would be cut and therefore the quality of its total service would deteriorate. RTE has "unrivalled and unique experience providing experimental community radio," said the document. This coupled with the RTE belief that "commercial local radio stations in major cities would not meet the real public demand," summed up the State broadcaster's pompous and seemingly watertight case for controlling local radio. While Dublin, Cork, Shannonside and "other densely populated areas", would probably be highly profitable, a lot of the sparsely populated countryside would not. Local radio was going to cost a lot of money before it started paying dividends and it was estimated that "the cost of the first stage of RTE local radio would put an extra 3% on the licence fee."

However tight the RTE argument may appear, it has its faults. The proposed community radio stations were to cater for areas of population ranging from 180,000 to 360,000. Within these regions would be smaller opt-out stations, operating on a rota system, in communities of around 3,000 people. These statistics concerning the population of catchment areas were only estimates. The British figures of 250,000 per local radio station were simply scaled down to suit the Irish situation, not a very scientific approach. What is more, RTE's head of audience research Tony Fahey considered the size of local radio audiences to be "a variable number. I take it that's something that can be negotiated politically."

However convincing the craw-thumping of RTE sounded, financial considerations would have prevented the State monopoly from operating the smaller rural stations, without also controlling those in larger centres of population. "I think this would be the doomsday kind of bad dream of senior executives in this organisation," said Tony Fahey, "that we'll get the unprofitable areas, in other words the real public service stuff, where nobody wants to go, like Leitrim. Nobody could ever make a shilling down in that place. While the profitable areas like Dublin are creamed off. That would be a disaster."

The RTE document does make one statement that the relevant Minister should have paid attention to. When discussing pending legislation, the RTE proposal warned that, "solutions adopted in the U.K. may not necessarily be the best for this country, although it may be tempting to follow their example." Not only did Minister Reynolds ignore the RTE proposal, he foolishly chose to ignore the warning.

It's ironic that the Irish Government attacked the problem of pirate radio when it did. Instead of smothering the creature at birth, the government waited until it had eaten the heroine and turned into a fire breathing dragon before tackling it. Moreover when the government finally did charge the creature, it tripped over its own sword. The Broadcasting and Wireless Telegraphy Bill, 1980, and the Independent Radio Authority Bill, 1981, were respectively drafted to put an end to the pirates and introduce independent local radio. In the end they did neither as the Fianna Fail government fell, and with it went Reynolds' proposed legislation.

Ireland has no national communications policy, which becomes obvious when the national broadcasting organisation is on its knees, and pirate stations run rampant on the airwaves, both due to government indifference. "No TD is going to waste more than ten minutes of his time with something like pirate radio," said ex-Caroline DJ Chris Cary. Sadly he was right, which might account for the fact that when legislation was finally cobbled together, it wasn't so much drafted as photocopied.

Reynolds' Bill to introduce local radio was little more than a copy of the 1973 British legislation on the subject, minus its amendments, giving us an Irish solution to an Irish problem. The proposed Independent Local Radio Authority would have been very similar to the British IBA. Therefore Reynolds was introducing a centralised, mammoth, hierarchical body to oversee the development of local radio, with Ministerial appointments to top positions. RTE's relationship to this new Authority was never even mentioned.

Even as the Reynolds Bill hit the paper shredder, pirate radio came of age with the arrival of the first superpirate, Sunshine Radio.

6

Another
Kettle
Of Fish

"I think I was more interested in the mechanics of radio than I was in being a Famous Disc Jockey."
Chris Cary, Managing Director, Radio Nova.

In the year following Radio 2's launch, more and more stations had taken to the air, like Downtown Community Radio, and Community Radio Dun Laoghaire in late July. A Radio Skyline Dublin operated from Blackrock, there was Northside Radio on 217, Radio Dublin Channel 2 on 235, and the more successful Southside Radio from the Victor Hotel.

Under the name 'Spangles Muldoon' Chris Cary came to Radio Caroline for the last few months and worked as DJ under station manager Admiral Robbie Dale (Robbie Robinson). Robbie remembers that during that period he saw a television programme on the Irish pirate radio scene. Cary (who had an outlet here for his computer shop organisation) also saw the programme. Brian McKenzie, a Dublin based colleague of Cary's, had often mentioned the Irish pirate situation to Chris, who had in turn been in touch with Robinson.

Chris Cary remembers arriving in Dublin in 1981 to find "local radio stations which were a bit pitiful". Robinson also remembers that his first impressions of the Dublin pirates were "shattering!" - "Because prior to us arriving here, Brian McKenzie told us about some of the very successful stations...things like 'operating out of luxury hotels etc.,' and so Brian picked us up at the airport and drove us down the airport road and stopped at the Crofton, and there was ARD...and this was the luxury hotel operation!" At this stage Paul Vincent, Dr. Don and Dave C. were running ARD (Radio 257 had changed its name back to ARD on April 5th), but Paul Vincent was very much a sleeping partner as Dave and Don made most of the decisions without consulting him. It was now nearly sixteen months since the advent of Radio 2 and the Dublin stations had picked up some momentum.

Two Pirates

If first impressions are the most striking it is no small wonder that Robbie Robinson was "shattered" with what he found at ARD. "We wandered down the back to an annex and there was a girl sitting behind a telephone picking her nails, looking like she needed a wash. However we asked for Dr. Don, he was-not there, then Dave C, she rang him, and I thought, 'well, we're in some sort of area here, and it's going to open up into an office and then studios'... Dave C eventually arrived... with that he opened a side door into a bedroom and there was the station transmitter laid out on the floor, in bits,the studio was standing next to it on eggboxes, and there was a disco deck, and a couple of old Gararrds and a few tape machines. I just couldn't believe it, because the feeder from the transmitter was going across the floor through the toilet, through a hole in the window and up to the aerial - and that was the most successful radio station at that stage!" Chris Cary has similar memories, though not as colourful. On seeing ARD Cary and Robinson were filled with confidence. "Well, we thought, if that's the successful station, we won't need an awful lot to do better!"

At this stage the two ex-Caroline disc jockeys had no fixed development plan. One idea was to start a new station from scratch, another was to take over an existing Dublin pirate. But the stations had fallen into a rut. Pending legislation, the advent of Radio 2, and increased competition had all contributed to the winding down of operations. The two pirates weren't too impressed with what they saw and so trode gently until they found a suitable station with which to become involved. That station was to be Southside.

Southside Radio was originally started by some school friends in Bray. The station was then moved to a caravan in DJ Mark Boland's back garden. But after the transmitter went missing in the dead of night, the station was moved to the basement of the Hotel Victor. The driving force behind Southside was Andrew Coffee (alias Paul Nicholas and Andy Ruane), with Joe Jackson handling sales. In the days before the superpirates, Southside Radio was easily the most popular pirate in the South of the capital. This had more to do with the cliquish attitude of Southsiders than the brilliance of the station. Southside Radio, and therefore Andrew Coffee, went from rags to riches every couple of weeks. As money was earned, it was spent in night-clubs and at parties. It was seldom re-invested.

Andrew Hanlon (alias Dave Johnson), who was a DJ with Southside even before his voice broke, remembers the station as "a real wreck of a place...The turntables were stuck in old boxes. The mixer was a five channel, £95 job...The monitor? Forget the monitor - We didn't have a monitor! We had a pair of headphones and that was it!" As all the other Dublin pirates were on the northside or in the city centre, there was no real competition and Southside proved very popular in the affluent bay area, a market that was totally underexploited.

However Robinson and Cary never did take out an interest in Southside. Why? According to Robbie "because of the worries, the apprehension that was shown by the young boys involved there, we didn't go ahead." At this time Paul Vincent was involved with Southside and he remembers that Coffee was ready to welcome Robinson and Cary "with open arms...they had more or less agreed that they would move in there, but when Andrew Coffee sat down beside the two of them and asked them where was his share, they decided that that wasn't on really and they pulled out." This version of the story is a lot more likely, as businessmen like Cary and Robinson tend not to be terribly chivalrous.

After their near involvement with Southside, the dynamic duo decided to go it alone. The search was on for a home for Sunshine Radio. Scherick Island off the coast of Skerries was considered, as was the Sands Hotel, then still under construction. A message had been communicated to Robbie and Chris from John Ryan, owner of the Sands, and the two pirates paid him a visit. Robbie remembers that on arriving at the hotel "....we were asked to wait for about ten minutes. John Ryan appeared. Ten minutes later the deal was signed, sealed and delivered." Paul Vincent recalls that before Robinson and Cary went to Sands, John Ryan, who is a personal friend of his, rang to ask advice on having a radio station on his property. Paul met Ryan and told him "that it would probably be in 'his interest to have it." The location was settled, the new station was to operate from the Sands Hotel, Portmarnock.

With the location settled, Robinson and Cary started to plan the Sunshine project. Using their vast experience as a yardstick the two pirates planned the station with meticulous precision. The studios would be custom built, the transmitter would be powerful and the disc jockeys professional. At this stage most of the finance for the station was coming from Cary and Phil Solomon, who put up 40% each. Chris casually recalls his investment "wasn't very much, about fifteen thousand pounds". The remaining 20% of the capital came in equal amounts from Robbie Robinson and the station engineer, Jim White.

The involvement of ex-Radio Caroline director Philip Solomon in the Sunshine affair is unusual. Robbie Robinson stated that when they approached Solomon about political contacts in this country "....he obviously wanted to know why we wanted to know. Chris told him and he said that he'd be interested in getting involved in the venture." Chris however remembers that after talking Robinson into becoming involved in Sunshine, "Robbie then must have felt that he owed something to this man Philip Solomon who was eventually brought into it...it was just my baby for months. I did all the jingles, all the format and everything at the beginning. Personally, I hope you don't let Robbie hear this, but I thought it sounded fucking good at the beginning. It had myself and Tony Allan, it was just quite a groovy station." A groovy station it may have been, but neither Cary nor Robinson seem to agree on how Solomon became involved in the project. This is not unusual as they never seem to see eye-to-eye on anything. The story that follows goes some way towards explaining why, and even on that they disagree.

Portmarnock Blues

On 14th September 1980 Robbie Robinson broadcast Sunshine Radio's first test transmission. It was a great success, with reception reports coming in from both Ireland and the UK. Everyone was happy, the long struggle to get the station on the air was over. At around 4 am that Monday morning, Sunshine's one hundred and sixty foot aerial mysteriously collapsed. At first it was thought that it had exploded, but in fact that impression was given by the falling aerial hitting electric wires and a water storage tank. Gardai released a statement saying that the aerial was felled by high winds not sabotage. But a Sunshine spokesman denied this saying, it "was certainly no accident". Robinson and Cary both agree, Robbie adding drily, "high winds, with metal cutters".

Whatever the cause of the aerial collapse, its consequences are much more important. Cary decided to leave Sunshine. If his 40% in the company was withdrawn, the whole project might well collapse as dramatically as the aerial had. Robinson however believed that Sunshine had a future, that the project was still viable and that Cary should stay. The two men were at odds as the discrepancy in their versions of what follows shows all too clearly. According to Robbie, "the aerial was chopped down, Chris pulled out, thought the whole thing was lunacy, dangerous, and got on the plane and flew back to London. Immediately Phil Solomon found out, he backed out."

But Cary remembers, "Sunshine was my baby, I got very excited about doing my own station. Now Robbie is very different from me, he has to be in charge-

and I was away all the time and every time I came back things had been changed and they were, I thought, changed for the worse...so I then went to Philip who owned half of the equity and said I want out... he said if you're gone, I'm gone!" Cary added that the vandalising of the aerial "was a bit of a nuisance", but it played no real part in his decision to pull out. Whatever the sequence of events leading up to Cary's departure from the Sunshine project, the end result was the same. With Cary and Solomon gone, 80% of Sunshine's £32,000 operating capital was gone too. It looked as if the sun wouldn't shine in Portmarnock for much longer.

According to Robinson seven days grace was given during which time he could buy up Chris's percentage of the equity. Solomon gave Robinson twenty-eight days. With that Robbie borrowed £25,000, using his house as collateral and paid off Cary and Major Barker Solomon. He therefore retained 90% of Sunshine's equity, the remaining 10% lying with station engineer Jim White.

With a lot of help from Sammy Prendergast of Prendergast Aerials, Sunshine Radio eventually took to the air on September 29th 1980. Within weeks advertising was coming into the station. At this stage Robbie was totally committed, he had no choice, everything he owned was riding on the success of the radio station. "I had confidence," he said "I had a lot more faith than confidence. I just believed the time was right, that the radio industry was going to start developing in a legal way, and as I had the experience I thought the only way I am going to get into the radio business in Ireland was to do it." So he did. Later others were to get financially involved with Sunshine. They included Jack O'Leary the former Dail superintendent and Dr. Kenneth Holden of the Central Remedial Clinic, whose wife Elizabeth ironically enough was a director of An Bord Telecom, half of the old Department of Posts and Telegraphs!

Robinson admits that in the prebroadcast stage Cary had planned to beam Sunshine into Britain. Even after the aerial collapse Solomon was telling the newspapers that Sunshine was not interested in advertising from the Dublin market, that the station was being aimed at the North of England. However with the departure of Solomon and Cary, Sunshine took on less ambitious targets. Mike Hogan, who joined Sunshine as an advertising sales-rep, took thirteen weeks to make his first sale, "to Lionel's Barber Shop, in Wicklow Street, for the princely total of £150". He got £22.50 commission. Robinson remembers that initially he too "was out selling fifty pound deals to local traders, so how do you take that sort of operation into the British market?' Cary though, who made his final broadcast on January 30th 1981, was to get one more bite at that lucrative cherry.

Decline and Growth

The reaction to Sunshine Radio was in the words of its Director Robbie Robinson, "very good, it became very popular, very quickly, because it was

The early Sunshine team

tight, it was far more professional than anything that was on the air then." The previous giants of pirate radio were in decline. Paul Vincent and Ian Dempsey had left ARD as the station slipped from being one of the the country's best pirates to being once more a back room operation. The Big D had been apathetic about broadcasting since the fire in Chapel Lane, and when the station moved to a closet under the stage of Ricardo's pool hall, morale dropped even further.

In a bid to stop the rot, James Dillon brought in Tony Johnson as a management consultant. "I gave him a completely free hand," said Dillon, but nothing worked. The attitude was wrong, sales weren't being made and disc jockeys often didn't turn up for work. In a desperate attempt to tighten the station's operation Johnson made some unpopular moves, like firing founding members Gerry Campbell, Tony Dixon and John Paul. He then hired in, for at the time sizeable salaries, Steve Rhodes, Jason Maine, Tony Fenton and Aidan Cooney. This however did little for morale or audience figures and by Christmas 1979 Dillon remembers "we were financially in a spot of bother." Down at The Big D they were thinking, "maybe we'll get another week of broadcasting out of it." Big D disc jockey Dennis Murray however believed that the station had a future. He convinced Dillon that an aggressive attitude was needed to pull the pirate out of the rut it had sunk into in Camden Street. Over the next two years Murray did everything he could to save the pirate, but to no avail. The superpirates had captured the Dublin market.

In late 1977 and early 1978, Radio Dublin was the nation's leading pirate station. It had introduced innovation after innovation which culminated in twenty four hour broadcasting. By 1980 however, the mighty 253 was in decline. The station was putting out the same format in 1980 as it had three years previously. The radio audience had matured, the Dublin stations hadn't. Sunshine Radio sounded different. For a start it had a record library and cart machines. Down at Radio Dublin the record library was pretty small, and there were plenty of accusations of payola. The unpaid Radio Dublin DJs would often tape Larry Gogan's Top Thirty programme on Radio 2 then mark in the points where a song started, play it on air and hope that they could fade out the music before Larry, Jimmy Greely or a Radio 2 jingle would blast out. Sometimes they didn't make it, but no one seemed to notice.

At this point too, Radio Dublin also pirated the start of the RTE Radio 1 News at 1.30. Again the DJ would have to anticipate the end of the headlines and cut in before Maurice O'Doherty launched into the bulletin. They usually made it, and the DJ's "Thanks a lot Maurice, that's all the news for now.." caused untold hilarity among the newscasters in RTE. The days of DJ Lee and smoochy Kevin Barrett were numbered.

Radio Telefís Éireann

Baile Átha Cliath 4, Éire   telefón 01–69 31 11, teleics 52 68
Dublin 4, Ireland   telephone 01–69 31 11, telex 52 68
20 May, 1981.

Mr. Eamon Cooke,
Director,
Radio Dublin,
3 Sarsfield Road,
Dublin 8.

Dear Mr. Cooke,

Thank you for your letter of 9 May informing us that Radio Dublin has ceased to re-broadcast the RTE 8.00 a.m. and lunchtime News as requested but that you are still transmitting the 6.30 p.m. News. Your request for permission to continue to re-broadcast the 6.30 p.m. News and the reasons which you have put forward in support of it have received very careful consideration. I have to inform you however that we find we are unable to grant the request.

"I don't like the idea of foreigners coming in and practically taking over the airwaves," said Eamon Cooke, adding that "the money is going out of the country, that's the worst part of it. In a way you can't blame them; if they make money here, they'll ship it home, get it on a plane every Friday morning." Robbie Robinson remembers that the reaction to Sunshine from the existing stations was to say the least cool. "There were lots of threats...verbal, on the phone and through the grapevine." He added that security was very heavy around the studios and the new aerial.

By late October 1980 advertising had picked up a lot on Sunshine, so much so that Aer Lingus booked time on the station in preference to RTE. The advertising came to Sunshine through an informal meeting that Robinson had with a "senior figure" in the airline. "He felt he wasn't getting to the young market, the 20-25 year olds. He listened to the station and booked advertising. It was as simple as that," explained Robinson. Simple or not, RTE weren't amused. By late 1980, the State broadcasting organisation was in deep financial trouble. A spokesman at the time stated that they deplored the Aer Lingus decision, "not on the advertising point, but because it is illegal and is making illegal use of the airwaves." This stiff upper lip approach was still being used by RTE up to 1982. In September of 1980 the station's Director General stated that the proliferation of pirate operations had not cost RTE a lot in lost advertising revenue, "we certainly have not lost out. They must be affecting the newspapers." By 1981 RTE was fighting for survival, with one hand tied behind its back. The station had meant to phase out drink advertisements, but the date was postponed. A spokesman at the time said "There has been no change in the authority's decision to phase out drink advertising, the timing has been deferred." This deferral bought RTE valuable time, and the lucrative contracts were to bring in much needed cash to help fill the rather depleted coffers down at Montrose.

RTE had another close encounter with advertisers in November, when the Army decided to launch an FCA recruitment campaign on Radio Dublin. When the Government heard of the Army's support for a pirate station it demanded that the ads be withdrawn at once. Cooke however said that was impossible as they had been scheduled and as every bureaucrat knows, a schedule cannot be changed. However he did offer to do his best when the FCA settled their account in full. This they did and the adverts stopped.

But Radio Dublin and its clones were on the decline. No other pirate station could match Sunshine Radio for signal strength or professionalism. Even though it would be another year before the station started 24 hour broadcasting, Sunshine was the talk of the town.

On April 14th a new and different station started operating from Dublin's Herbert Street. It was Radio Leinster. Initially to be called Happy Radio, Leinster aimed at an older audience. But Leinster's middle of the road output could never match that of RTE Radio 1, and the station was in constant financial trouble. In time it slipped from producing average programmes to producing mediocre rubbish.

Other minor operations scattered around the capital at this time included: H-Block Radio on 248, which came on air in December, Dublin Community Radio on 312 which opened a month earlier and the Alternative Broadcasting Channel, which opened at 9pm on November 1st 1981.

Night Moves

One of the more successful programmes on Radio 2 was Night Moves, presented by Declan Meehan and produced by his old pal, Mark Storey. While it attracted a huge audience Declan was very unhappy in RTE. On the music side, he resented playing "all that Brendan Shine rubbish", and he couldn't understand RTE's stilted view of broadcasting - "It's like a priest running a disco," he said. According to Declan even a simple task was complicated in RTE. "You'd have to book a studio, get a sound engineer, get a disc man, get a producer...and it takes all these people in the one place, just to put a record on tape...it was just dreadful."

Initially Declan was in awe of those in RTE, but when he first saw his name beside Gay Byrne's in the *RTE Guide*, it all became very ordinary. "The first morning I was there, I was giving a time check and I said, 'it's 19 after 8' - and I was told: 'You don't say 19 after 8 on RTE, you say nineteen minutes after eight o'clock.'" Then Declan's outspoken views on the RTE bureaucracy became well known within the station. "Louis Hogan rang me up one Saturday morning and said, 'we're discussing the new schedule, can I see you?' So I went around to his house and he said, 'the news actually isn't very good Declan, you're not on the next schedule.' I said, 'why not Louis, you know how successful the programme is', 'yeah' he says 'but we're dropping the programme...we have to keep an eye to commercial radio, so we want an easy listening programme at night.'"

Declan admitted he was disappointed when his contract was not renewed, but "a month before, Chris Cary and Robbie Dale had arrived in town and set up Sunshine Radio, so I went to Sunshine." "I didn't know him from Adam," admitted Robbie "but his reputation preceded him, so I gave him a job." Declan Meehan was now working for Sunshine. It was late 1980.

The in-fighting between Radio 257, Big D and Radio Dublin was temporarily forgotten in February 1981. It was after the disastrous fire where 48 young people died at a Valentine's party in the Stardust Club. On the invitation of 257, Radio Dublin and The Big D picked up the signal from the Crofton and relayed 257's coverage of the funeral mass from Beaumont. It was sad that it took a tragedy like the Stardust to bring the three Dublin stations together - even then, it was just for the day.

The Politics of Dancing

On Wednesday April 22nd 1981, the Radio City studios in Capel Street were occupied by supporters of the Hunger Strike. At 11.45 am on Sunday May 3rd, two days before the death of hunger striker Bobby Sands, a group of twenty or so youths chanting H-Block slogans attacked and tried to occupy Radio Dublin. Eamon Cooke remembers that the H-Block supporters "just smashed their way in, dug holes in the floor, emptied the fridge and carried on like animals." The protesters demanded air time on the station, which Cooke refused. Ironically H-Block radio was back on the air, "so why on earth did they want to take over everybody else?" asked Cooke. The Gardai finally arrived and the pro-hunger strikers "were allowed to walk out of the place, march down the road as if nothing had happened."

This wasn't to be the last time that politics and pirate radio were to meet. With the fall of the Fianna Fail government a General Election was called, and during the month of June, much to the annoyance of RTE, politicians from all the major parties were to be found broadcasting on the pirate airwaves. "You can't ridicule the politicians for getting involved with Sunshine," said Robinson, "we acquired a very large audience...so when the 1981 general election came about, it wasn't surprising that we were approached by local TDs."

Some of the Fianna Fail politicians to use the pirates during that election campaign were Liam Lawlor, Gerard Brady, Michael Donnelly, Jim Tunney and Sean Moore. At the time Fianna Fail claimed to have "no official contact with pirate stations - they're all outside the law." That statement was released by Fianna Fail worker and RTE country music DJ Paschal Mooney. At the same time that Mooney was saying this, John Stephenson, a Fianna Fail information officer was booking advertising time on the pirate stations and encouraging young people to vote for Fianna Fail: "Don't let Garrett and Frank fool you..." was how one advert began. In the end it was Fianna Fail who were fooling themselves.

On the other side of the fence, Fine Gael had no hesitation in broadcasting on pirate radio, "we're using them in relation to our youth policy" claimed Fine Gael worker and RTE sports commentator Bill O'Herlihy. Only the Labour Party refrained from using the capitalist commercial pirates - although not for ideological reasons, a spokesman tried to explain: "There's nothing in principle against it as far as we're concerned, it's just that we don't have the money."

The hypocritical attitude of all the major parties followed decades of inaction on the subject of broadcasting. The pirates were useful at election time and the chaos on the airwaves and RTE's deep financial problems were less important than winning seats in the Dail.

While in office Fianna Fail had brought forward the farcical Reynolds Bill, which if implemented would have discouraged Independent Local Radio. Fine Gael were in two minds about the whole subject and the Labour Party had sold its soul to commercialism by offering politicians, free of charge, to the pirates. Amid all this political opportunism and indecision, Sunshine Radio introduced an equal-time rota. Each party would be given an opportunity to make a party political broadcast, and advertisements could be placed at 50% of the normal rate-card price. This unprecedented move, and the willing co-operation of the politicians, gave Sunshine the type of credibility money can't buy. Eamon Cooke summed up his feelings on the double standards of Irish politicians: "They all like to use us to get their own point across on the airwaves. But when it comes to giving us a licence, that's another kettle of fish."

After the election, a coalition of Fine Gael and Labour took office. But they weren't to remain in power for long. Two more General Elections followed in quick succession, ensuring political instability, the perfect compost for growing pirate radio stations.

7

Hamburger Radio

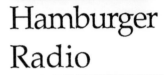

"'Community' is one of these elastic, political words that can mean whatever you want it to mean."
Tony Fahy, Head of Information, RTE.

Most of the seventy or so stations scattered around the country in mid-1981 were commercial. They played non-stop music and tried to make money. But there was a second type: Community Radio. These operations were far less numerous than their commercial cousins, and included: Tipperary Community Radio; Carlow Community Radio; Kilkenny Community Radio and Bray Local Broadcast. As

The summer of 1981 saw another boom in the number of pirate stations operating. In Dublin alone there was Radio Diamond on 189; Westside on 195; Railway Road on 290; Radio Pandora which opened on June 30th, and on 212 metres Premier Radio International. But the most interesting of all was a mystery station, with a crystal clear signal, operating from Green Acres, Rathfarnham.

time went by many other stations adopted the title 'Community'; however most of them weren't. They were just looking for sympathy.

So what is the difference between a community and a commercial radio station?

To qualify as a 'community' station, the broadcasts must be decentralised and de-commercialised. The station must serve a recognisable, pre-existing community. The station must have a non-profit making democratic structure that encourages participation from all sectors of the community, and the station in return must try to appeal to all sectors of the community with predominantly locally originated programming.

To qualify as a 'commercial' station, programmes must be of mass appeal and therefore notions of 'social responsibility' would be missing or be very peripheral, since first priority must go to advertisers. The stations would aim to be profit making and would be independent of any strict governmental control on the operating structures of the station. No financing should come directly from the public purse.

The very great difference between community and commercial radio was often fudged by politicians and RTE. For example, on 7th May 1981, The Joint Committee on State Sponsored Bodies released a report on RTE. In the document they defined commercial (local) radio, and community radio:

Local Radio: Professionally operated studios, located in sizeable urban areas, offering items of interest to their local audiences probably heavily funded by advertising revenue.

Community Radio: A socially very commendable enterprise pioneered by RTE which gives community groups responsibility for the preparation and presentation of programmes under the guidance and editorial control of regional RTE staff.

In the light of RTE's evidence to the committee and because of predictions made by RTE's Director General that "... if independent local radio is licensed in Dublin City alone....it will cost RTE between £1.5 million and £2 million per annum," the committee decided that independent commercial radio would not be suited to Irish needs and therefore "The committee supports RTE's plans for the provision of community radio."

But that was community radio as set out in the report "socially very commendable....pioneered by RTE". Couldn't community radio be run independently of the State broadcaster? It may be naive, but one would have expected the Joint Committee to define what they were talking about. Without correct information, a proper conclusion cannot be reached. And the definitions used by the committee were weighted, grossly biased and totally inadequate.

Professional Elitism

In the early days of the BBC monopoly (and therefore the RTE monopoly), the public were given what was good for them - high culture. Pop culture was a dirty word and unworthy of valuable air-time. As we have seen, all this changed with the arrival of Radio Caroline, a truly commercial station. With the notion of 'social responsibility' absent, Caroline (and in Ireland Nova *et al*) went after the mass youth market. They did this very successfully and made a lot of money. The very success of these stations shows they were answering a public need. Or does it?

Those in favour of community radio believe that the answer is 'no'. In their opinion the only stations that answer a public need are those set up by the public. Commercial stations are primarily for the benefit of advertisers, the public come a poor second. The argument continues that commercial stations are popular only because there is no real choice. Community radio appeals by definition to a much smaller population than something commercial. This therefore makes the total number of listeners to any individual community station tiny in comparison to those tuned to a commercial operation.

Founded in 1983, The National Association of Community Broadcasting (NACB), was constantly to the fore in making the case for 'Community Access Radio'. "At the moment the NACB ... merely acts as a lobbying group and a means by which community activists could actually talk to politicians", said the Association's Development Officer, Sally Reynolds. The NACB's 10 point charter sums up the organisation's philosophy and all member stations had to abide by it. By early 1988, there were 9 such community stations on air. "The only thing that we expect from our members is that they sign

N.A.C.B. CHARTER

Community Broadcasting should:

1. Serve recognisable local geographic communities and communities of interest.

2. Ensure that democratic ownership and control rests within the local community or community of interest.

3. Be a non-profit distributing trust, co-operative or similar registered structure and have a commitment to the use of surplus funds for community development work.

4. Have its general management and programming policy made by a governing committee which is democratically representative of the people of the recognisable local community and the various interests of the community.

5. Provide within this democratic structure, a service of information education and entertainment and enable the two-way communication of diverse opinions and provide a "right of reply" to any person or organisation subject to serious misrepresentation.

6. Be financed from resources generated by the local community, including advertising.

7. Be committed to providing local people with access to training, production and transmitting facilities.

8. Endeavour to transmit programme material that is predominantly locally originated.

9. Ensure that the Irish language and culture are adequately represented.

10. Have a programming policy which encourages the development of a participatory democracy and which is opposed to racism, sexism, and any other discriminatory attitudes, as well as undertaking to provide equal employment opportunities.

and agree to abide by that charter. Now how they do radio after that, once they stick to those ideals, is up to them."

The NACB did not actually represent any of its member stations, as the association itself was quite legal, whereas unlicensed broadcasting was not. To add to the confusion, the association's development officer Sally Reynolds was being paid by the taxpayer via the Youth Employment Agency (YEA). This led to numerous complications as the Department of Labour, who operated the YEA, could not be seen to support an illegal activity - like pirate broadcasting.

• • •

Bray Local Broadcast (BLB) was very much the darling station in the NACB family. Since 1979 the station had pioneered community access radio. On BLB community groups produced a wide and varied range of programming from local drama to classical music to heavy metal. This schedule was supplemented by disc jockey type shows and around 17% speech content, made up of community news desks and information supplied by locals. Sally Reynolds, who was manager of BLB for 3 years explains: "There are different levels of access. Access at its most simple is the fact that a local community group can get its message read out once a week. At the other end of the scale it's when a local group actually comes in, is taught how to use the facilities and makes the pro-

BLB in action on Sunday 5th July 1987 at Bray Seaside Festival.
Station Manager Adrian Kennedy sunbathes topless by the caravan.

gramme itself." Programmes can be made by communities with a common interest (drama, golf, civil defence) or by geographical communities. Either way broadcasts are always made by volunteers, not professionals. Fr. Jerry Joyce of Kilkenny Community Radio (KCR) explained, "If we had a professional, the professional's task is not to broadcast, but to assist me, Joe Soap, to broadcast. Anything else is censorship by professional elitism."

"Out of Bray we've 120 volunteers - people who do three hours a day, five days a week. People who do an hour a week answering telephones", said BLB general manager Adrian Kennedy. For community radio to work properly, control must rest with the community and not with individuals. This is why many successful stations around the world are based on the principle and structure of the co-op. When private and personal gain gets in the way a community station can so easily collapse. Sally Reynolds explains, "Kilkenny Community Radio started the same time BLB did. And unlike BLB, they had commercial funding. A couple of local businessmen in the area genuinely put money into the station, they wanted to help get a station started. So it was a combination of commercial and community interests. It worked fine for a couple of years, but then the inevitable struggle broke out because the commercial guys wanted to maximise their money, they wanted to get a return on what they'd actually put in - they wanted a simple programming format, they were not happy with the community side of it."

The end result was the collapse of KCR with the community lobby group establishing the Kilkenny Community Communications Co-operative (KCCC) and raising £40,000 through the sale of shares. This money was to be put into a new station. Community stations, like their bigger commercial bedfellows, are ultimately controlled by market forces. Financial feasability then is very important and the NACB are confident that their stations can survive in the harsh and competitive marketplace, "We can be just as competitive as a commercial outfit" explained Sally Reynolds, "....in fact we can be far more competitive because obviously we can use volunteers. We would argue that a commercial station has no business using volunteers."

Community radio stations were a rare breed, but where they did exist the clergy (as with Fr. Jerry Joyce and Fr. Liam Carroll of Kilkenny Community Radio) were often behind the venture. The church had long taken an interest in the potential of radio. The Catholic Communications Centre, Booterstown, ran Ireland's first courses in local radio. It also ran other media participation projects mainly for the religious community, both at home and abroad. But whatever was to happen with local radio, the type of stations the Church wished for were about as far away as you can get from what was to happen next!

Clutter Free

After Robinson successfully re-launched Sunshine Radio, Chris Cary wanted to buy his way back in. Robinson refused. Cary had been very busy with his computer business. He had acquired a licence to manufacture Sinclair computers for the American market and in his words "we fucking printed money off it, I didn't need a radio station, this thing was making me thousands of dollars a day." As well as being fabulously rich, Cary is also fabulously modest. Brian McKenzie, Cary's man in Dublin, had been keeping an eye on the Irish radio scene. He, and others, contacted Chris in London to give a run down on how Sunshine was doing.

According to Cary, they said that Robinson was raking in the money and that "this guy is driving us mad. He's bad-mouthing you all over town saying you couldn't do it, that you ran away from Ireland." Robinson dismisses this as pure fantasy. Finally through a mixture of boredom and disbelief, "I spent a hundred thousand pounds on equipment, I had it all flown to Ireland, I didn't even have an address, it was all flown to a shipping agent." Chris Cary then flew to Dublin to find a suitable "smart building" in which to house his new station. Brian McKenzie found such a place in a Georgian house in posh Herbert Street (just down the road from the struggling Radio Leinster, and above his Bay City Studios) with a rent of £600 a week. "We got the keys of the place, the equipment arrived three days later, we picked out the rooms where we wanted things, we fitted it all in and Nova was born."

There were numerous rumours floating around about Cary's Radio Nova. One was that the medium wave output from the station would be on board a ship bobbing up and down on the Irish Sea. Another that Radio Nova was to go nationwide, while more said the station would carry half its programmes in the Irish language! One of the funniest stories told of a broke Cary borrowing £300 from his girlfriend to launch the station! A lot of the conflicting reports about Nova stem from the same source - Chris Cary. Robbie Robinson summed up this facet of Chris's personality best: "He feeds all of these stories into the system. He sows all the seeds and then allows the acres to blossom." A lot of acres were to blossom over the next few years, and the stories were ultimately to contribute in no small way to more raids and Cary's eventual departure from these dollar-green shores.

Radio Nova's first 'official' broadcast was on 12th June 1981, when 88 FM boomed out 'clutter free' across Dublin City. "I think from day one," said Cary, "it just jumped out of people's radios." One person who wasn't too pleased about Chris' return was Robbie Robinson. The frequency of 88 FM was to be used by Sunshine. "When Nova arrived, they came up on 88 FM , because that was Sunshine's plan. Chris Cary was aware of the development ideas, obviously he was part and parcel of the early thing - 539 medium wave, switch down to

FM and you've got 88! We were very annoyed when he came up on that frequency. He was obviously using a confidence to his own advantage." A fact that didn't bother Chris in the least.

Around mid-May the country and western station Treble TR moved to Gene Brady's 'Green Acres' complex. The station had only 250 watts of power, but from its vantage point, the signal was reaching the west coast of Britain. Word of this got to Chris Cary who went to track down the site. Jimmy Smith, owner of Treble T.R. takes up the story. "I went up early in the morning to open the station at half seven...and I saw this colossal big aerial lying out in the car-park, and I though, 'that's nice, somebody's bestowing a mast upon me!' I discovered, when I asked questions, that there was another station movin' into Green Acres - Nova!" The two totally different stations operated alongside for several months while the Nova engineers perfected the microwave link which was to connect the studios in town to the transmitter in Rathfarnham. On 11th September 1981, while still at Green Acres, Nova started broadcasting on 846

Chris Cary behind the microphone

AM with the largest pirate medium wave transmitter in Ireland. This move "helped make us enormous" said Chris, and he wasn't too far wrong. As time went on Nova's 10Kw of power was seeping into the 250 watt signal of Treble TR. So the latter station moved to Walkinstown and in Jimmy Smith's words:

"They were clutter free Nova, we were Nova free Treble TR!" Shortly after this the microwave link was perfected and Nova moved to Herbert Street.

Pirate TV

June 1981 saw the birth of Dublin's first pirate television station. There had been a few attempts at pirate TV before this, like Boyneside TV, which if nothing else was notable for its longevity. Channel 3, or Channel D, as it was later to be called, had one thing in common with Boyneside TV - it too failed.

Behind the venture were Dr. Don and Michael Tiernan of the Mickey Mouse organisation, the NIBO. Operating from Phibsboro in Dublin, Channel D began test transmissions in early June but only broadcast periodically until Thursday August 20th, when it returned with a fanfare, broadcasting in colour. Don Moore announced to the press that he was confident the station would attract thousands of viewers. That day's programmes consisted of *Dublin Profile*, a magazine show with a piece about the Samaritans, and music from The Sussed. The adverts were from a video shop, Zhivago's nightclub and a kilt manufacturer! Channel D returned the following Thursday at 3.20pm. It showed the same edition of *Dublin Profile* as before, and left the air at 5.30pm. It was also on the next day, with the same programme. The pirate continued infrequent broadcasts, repeating the now threadbare Dublin Profile, until September 2nd when the station announced that it was to commence breakfast TV from 9.30am to 11.30am, with films each evening!

Predictably, breakfast TV never materialised, and people began to wish that the films hadn't either. All through September Channel D broadcast such celluloid gems as *The Florida Connection; Silent Night, Bloody Night; White Comanchie; Aliens from Space-Ship Earth; Panic City* and the classic, *Children Shouldn't Play with Dead Things*. All that was missing from this 'B-Movie' hall of fame were some old Ronald Reagan movies and *The Attack of the Killer Tomatoes*! After mid-October the pirate television station broadcast very irregularly, showing and re-showing the above dusty classics. Michael Tiernan, it would appear, didn't appreciate how difficult it is to make good television. It certainly can't be done on a shoestring budget and Channel D never won over the hearts of Dubliners, spoilt for choice with one of the highest concentrations of Cable TV in Europe. By the end of October, Channel D, like the old cinema it operated from, had become defunct.

1981 was rife with talk of pirate television. Not to be outdone Chris Cary started circulating rumours of Nova TV. "We wouldn't be competing with RTE, because Nova intends to launch breakfast TV, and beat Britain to it....it's the logical development for a successful radio station to branch out into television," he added nonchalantly.

As 1981 drew to a close the Minister for Posts and Telegraphs Patrick Cooney promised legislation to combat the pirate broadcasters. It would be introduced, that's right, in the next Dail session!

Yesterday's Flavours

The popularity of radio stations, like the popularity of the music they play, is governed by the tastes of a fickle audience. With the advent of Sunshine and Nova, listeners deserted Radio Dublin, The Big D and ARD. "Radio is a bit like fashion," said James Dillon, "and the Dublin stations had gone out of fashion. Without listening, people were saying, 'aah it takes Nova and Sunshine, they really know what they're doing!' People have said to me, 'pity you haven't the disc jockeys that Nova have!' But they were all the same disc jockeys! So there must have been something wrong with the format." Nova's format was different to any other station in Ireland. Music was to the forefront and waffle on the airwaves was forbidden. Broadcaster Peter Maddison was fired from Nova for

talking too much between records. "I sacked people," confirmed Cary "and I would do it again if they refused to obey the order to say nothing if there is nothing worthwhile to say." The other factor that helped make Nova a success was the strength of their signal.

When Radio Dublin introduced their new transmitter back in Christmas 1977, a whole new audience tuned into pirate radio. The station had captured the imagination of the public and radio would never be the same again. When Radio Nova introduced their new 10Kw rig, it had a similar effect. It opened up a new dimension in pirate broadcasting because their transmitter was as large as that used by RTE in the Dublin area, the most lucrative advertising market in the country.

But in 1981 it was the smaller stations that were feeling the pinch. It had always been the case that the station with the strongest signal had the largest listenership. There had never been an exception to this rule in Dublin. First Radio Dublin commanded the audience, then ARD, then The Big D, then Sunshine. When Nova came, Sunshine was pushed into second position, and the older Dublin stations dropped back further. James Dillon recalls that "small listenership leads to small advertising, leads to small thinking." The Big D moved premises, again with a short lease; then in December 1981 the itinerant station reached a new low. "Our standard of broadcasting had dropped," said James "and Nova had caught on." The station staff were dissatisfied, all the good DJs were with the paying Sunshine and Nova and the general opinion of the Dublin stations was that they were a load of waffle!" In December 1981, The Big D closed down. It had been broadcasting twenty four hours a day since April 1978.

Nova, on the other hand with its superior signal, was all set for a prosperous 1982. "Someone has accused us of being a hamburger station," Chris told newspapers in late December, "that doesn't offend me. For instance you can go into McDonalds anywhere in the world and you know you will get a certain type of food...that is what Radio Nova is for. Instantly recognisable sound, suitable for a couple of hours listening. No-one was providing this sort of service."

The
Plot
Thickens

*"Nine out of ten people in pirate radio are
gay. The other ten per cent are liars."*
Tony Allan, veteran pirate broadcaster.

1982 proved to be an eventful year in the
pirate radio world. It saw the larger, more professional stations consolidate their position in
the market, while seriously threatening that of
RTE. It also saw a boom in the number of smaller stations operating, many of which collapsed,
to be replaced by yet more. During a politically
unstable year, the pirates were never in any serious danger of closure, and indeed one political
party took it upon itself to jump on the band-
wagon.

Cork Broadcasting Company,
Alternative Broadcasting Cork,
Community Radio Cork, Capital
Radio Cork, Leeside Radio,
Cork City Local Radio, Radio
Caroline, Cork and Radio City
were the stations of the early
pirate era in the nation's second
city. Stations around County
Cork included: North Cork Local
from the Majestic Ballroom,
Community Radio Youghal,
Middleton Community Radio
and East Side Radio, from the
seaside resort of Ballycotton.

Designer Radio

During the summer holidays of May 1980, seventeen year old schoolboy Joe O'Connor set up his own radio station "just for tricks". The station was called Cork Eastside Radio and operated on FM from the O'Connor's holiday home. Without searching for it, advertising slowly began to creep into the hobby station - enough to swell the wallets of all the family members.

The O'Connor family own Progress Engineering and other highly lucrative enterprises. Joe, their son, wanted success "big and quickly" so, with him prodding at his parents, they invested a substantial amount in the hobby station, bought a medium wave transmitter and called in Radio Boyneside's Eric Vaughan. Station engineer Paul Graham remembers that Eric "was impressed with the amount of money that could be produced." So Vaughan took the helm, introduced "semi-professional" disc jockeys and renamed the station Eastside Radio.

By the end of Summer 1982, Eastside Radio was chugging along, using jingles from Radio City, Dublin, cut to suit. The quality was poor but the prospects were good. Paul remembers that Cork had never before had a good station, so advertising came in quickly. Recognising radio as a good investment, the O'Connor family moved the station to their home, just outside Cork City. Two 'Portacabin' prefabs were built, a 5Kw transmitter was introduced and ex-RNI engineer Robin Banks joined the station. It was November 1982; £1,000 was spent on American-made jingles and the station was renamed ERI (Enterprise Radio Ireland). By Christmas 1982, ERI was beginning to capture more and more listeners, "we find that in Munster, apart from Radio 2, there's only ourselves to listen to," said Paul Graham. But there was a second big money pirate in Cork, which was also claiming to be the leader in the city. That second station was South Coast Radio.

Radio City Cork was a modest little station going nowhere terribly quickly. Peter O'Neill and Peter Maher had heard Sunshine and Nova, liked the sound and felt that they could do the job as well, down South. They left City and with the financial backing of local businessmen set up South Coast Radio. For the first year the station operated on a modest 1Kw transmitter, but, recalls Tony Allan, they wanted to "run the thing as a business rather than as a Mickey Mouse operation." South Coast got off the ground very quickly and soon invested in a 10Kw transmitter, giving it, along with Nova, the largest pirate output in the country.

Both ERI and South Coast were very popular in Cork throughout 1982, but, according to Paul Graham, "we were being jammed by RTE constantly...from Spur Hill...the man there is Bob Law...he jams South Coast on FM with white noise, and he jams us with a small 50 watt transmitter off channel." Commenting on the jamming, the eighteen year old Managing Director of ERI, Joe O'Connor, stated that, "We have dealt with this in a diplomatic way..." Just what "diplomatic" channels Mr. O'Connor used can only be guessed at. But the family do have strong Fianna Fail connections. This same political 'jobbery' was in evidence in 1983, when the subject of a licence was discussed with a senior person from the station. "We're all sworn to secrecy," the author was told, "...if Fianna Fail were in power, things would be a lot different. Nobody can guarantee a licence, but we have fairly good indications we would be amongst the top three or four in Ireland to be considered." The mere mortals in other stations would have to apply for a licence through more normal channels.

In Dublin, the first big news of 1982 was the return of The Big D, with James Dillon behind a new automatic format of DJ-less, non-stop music. The station recommenced broadcasting on 273 metres on January 17th, in the middle of the coldest winter for over fifty years. Ten days later the Coalition Government fell when their budget proposals were rejected, and yet another General Election was called. Fianna Fail were to get back into power for a short eight months, but not before some of the most amazing, and as yet undocumented events in the whole farcical history of political involvement in pirate radio were to take place.

A Fiasco

On 10th February 1982, eight days before the General Election, the weekly *Southside* newspaper carried an unprecedented advertisement in support of Fianna Fail. It was "placed by the friends and employees of Sunshine Radio," and read: "If you love your local unlicensed radio station vote Fianna Fail."

The Irish national broadcasting service is bound by statute to be fair and unbiased on political matters. The Sunshine Radio pro-

In the pirate television world, Boyneside TV accused RTE of jamming their signal. Eobhain McDonnell was quoted as saying that an RTE van "....Put out a signal which blanked us out in some areas of the town." In fact the RTE van was acting as a transposer, in that it boosted the RTE signal in Drogheda and thus the weaker Boyneside signal was drowned out.

On March 18th, programming at Radio Leinster went automatic. After all the presenters had said their farewells, the station went after its share of the lucrative youth market, only to revert to its old format after a few uneventful weeks of automated broadcasting.

IF YOU LOVE YOUR
LOCAL UNLICENCED
RADIO STATION

Vote for Your Valentine

VOTE Fianna Fáil

Fianna Fáil is the only party who have given
a Firm commitment to the introduction of

INDEPENDENT COMMERCIAL RADIO

*THIS IS THE ONLY CHANCE YOUR RADIO
STATION HAS OF GETTING A LICENCE*

This advertisement has been placed by friends and employees of Sunshine Radio

Fianna Fail campaign then was unprecedented. Never before had an Irish broadcasting channel, licensed or unlicensed, openly supported one political party at the expense of another. The advertisement "had absolutely nothing to do with party politics," stressed a cautious Robbie Robinson. "We were saying vote for independent radio, and Fianna Fail had a bill, and there it was, in black and white...I then looked at Fine Gael and they had nothing...The Labour Party were totally opposed. I then looked at all the possibilities - they were a return of Fianna Fail or a Coalition. The Coalition would be made up of a party that was totally opposed and a party that had no plans, and so what I said was, if you want independent radio, then vote for the party who are proposing independent radio."

However well reasoned that argument may sound, it still does not hide the fact that Robinson used Sunshine to disseminate his own political beliefs. With this move, Sunshine put themselves firmly in the Fianna Fail camp. "Lobbying lends to your credibility," said Robbie, adding that he felt political connections were "vitally important". Mike Hogan, who had at this stage left Sunshine for Radio Nova, felt that Robbie's canvassing was "totally wrong...Many people have been of the opinion that if you keep your bib clean and you do all the right things, somebody will eventually turn around and hand you a licence -

I'm not too sure that that's going to be the way at all." Only time would tell whether Robinson or Hogan was right.

Robbie Robinson was not wholly to blame for running the advertisement in *Southside*, or indeed, for repeating it in the *Sunday World*. The people to blame were the anonymous faces hiding behind the political smokescreen of Fianna Fail. However misdirected the Sunshine campaign was, it came as the direct result of communications from Fianna Fail. More or less the same communications Eamon Cooke received in early February.

On Monday February 15th, three days before the election, a new station started test broadcasts on 102 FM, blocking out Big D Automatic. The following day the pirate announced itself as Election Radio 1982. The new channel played plenty of Fianna Fail promotional tapes, which were also being broadcast by the other stations, but the most unusual thing about this pirate was its location - Fianna Fail election headquarters in the centre of Dublin. "We set it up in O'Connell Street for Fianna Fail," confirmed Eamon Cooke, "it was one of these things we just set up because it did appear that they were going to do something about radio."

Whatever Fianna Fail were saying to the pirates must have been very convincing. Two ex-Radio Dublin disc jockeys arranged all the technical details: Adrian St. James and John Paul (Patten) hired the stereo double decks, under assumed names, from Sound Hire Limited in Ranelagh. The decks were returned damaged. Both disc jockeys were actively involved in the Fianna Fail party and since the station was situated in election headquarters, it must have received the blessing of the highest echelons within the party.

With the Coalition out of office and Fianna Fail back in power, the pirates awaited their booty. If they expected it to come in the shape of a broadcasting licence, then the buccaneers were to be sorely disappointed. Not only were licences not forthcoming, but by June the Taoiseach Charles J. Haughey was saying that he deplored members of his party participating in pirate radio programmes!

But the technically illegal pirate stations were tolerated by consecutive Irish governments - that is, as long as they stuck to playing music and didn't threaten the status quo. RTE is bound by Section 31(1) of the Broadcasting Authority Act 1960 not to interview members of proscribed organisations, e.g. the IRA. In December 1982 Radio Leinster producer Gavin Duffy announced that he would be interviewing two Sinn Fein members, Danny Morrison and Gerry Adams. The Department of Posts and Telegraphs wrote to the station explaining that it would be a criminal offence to do so, and would militate against their chances of getting a licence. Justin James, station manager, assured the government that no such broadcast would take place, and for further conviction Radio Leinster fired Duffy.

The Numbers Game

Dublin's pirate radio scene was about to become more controversial than ever, with the release of audience figures from Radio Nova and RTE. Up to the summer of 1982, pirate stations tended not to conduct scientific audience research. The Big D was, in its day, one of the country's leading stations, yet it carried no certified listenership statistics. Rather, on the back of its late 1978 rate card it stated: "Results of a national poll, carried out by a well known pop journal, showed that Big D is the most listened to commercial radio station in Ireland!"

Therefore Radio Nova's commissioned audience research was one of the first of its kind. It showed that Radio 2 had 24% of the Dublin market, while Radio Nova had a 41% share. The RTE survey put the Radio 2 share at 46%; Radio Nova's share was not made explicit, but with 71% of Dublin's younger adults tuned to Radios 1 and 2, this would leave only 29% of the market between Radio Nova, Sunshine Radio, Radio Luxemburg, all the BBC stations and the remainder of the Dublin pirates. Something, somewhere was terribly wrong. The research results were important because prospective advertisers in the lucrative Dublin area would tend to place their contracts with the station claiming the largest audience. If this station was Nova, then the hard pressed Radio 2 could well lose most of its Dublin ad contracts and therefore, a large chunk of its revenue.

One of the research surveys had to be invalid, and both of them could have been. The RTE survey was conducted by the Market Research Bureau of Ireland (MRBI) during late March/early April 1982. The Radio Nova survey was commissioned from Lansdowne Market Research and was conducted in May/June of the same year. The differing dates of the polls should have made very little difference. What did make the difference then, according to Jack Jones of MRBI, was "the in-street interviewing technique" used by Lansdowne. "This is the first occasion in which published radio audience figures were based on this technique." The traditional method of interviewing people in the home was used in the MRBI/RTE poll.

While the Nova audience research was being carried out, the station was running a promotion. It was quite simple really - if someone stopped you in the street and asked what station you listened to, the word 'Nova' would win you ten pounds! Jack Jones of MRBI takes up the story, "Listeners were asked to look out for girls in public places"; these public places were also used conducting the survey. He continued that the girls "would ask...whether or not they had listened to Radio Nova. Cash prizes were offered to those who answered, 'Yes' to this and the follow-up questions. Our investigations show that many young people were hoping and waiting to be asked...Such a campaign...renders the entire Nova research project invalid."

The two surveys were presented to the Marketing Society for arbitration. After months of careful examination, the Society agreed with Jones. The Nova research was inaccurate due to the fact that a promotional campaign was being conducted at the same time as the poll. But the Society forbade both RTE and Nova from using the results of their respective surveys.

The Nova research findings did prove one thing - just how threatened RTE felt. Within two weeks of the Nova survey leaking to the press, the station was being jammed, as was Sunshine. Since moving back to Herbert Street, Radio Nova sent its signal to the transmitter in Rathfarnham via a sophisticated microwave link. On 29th June 1982, between 4.30pm and 5pm, that link was being interrupted on VHF. Nova blamed RTE, who of course denied the charge. Radio Nova engineers traced the source of the jamming to Rathmines and to an array of aerials on top of the RTE broadcasting museum. "We did signal tests last night and have absolutely no doubt at all that the jamming was caused by the mast," a Nova spokesman told the press at the time. Eamon Cooke also examined the aerials and explained that any signal on UHF cutting across the Nova link would effectively jam the pirate. The RTE aerials in Rathmines did face Rathfarnham, but whether RTE or the Department of Posts and Telegraphs were jamming Nova will remain unproveable for quite a while yet.

Only The Strong Survive

1982 was a fairly lean year for advertising, yet Sunshine and Nova got a large slice of whatever contracts existed. This didn't do much to encourage smaller stations which began to fold in ever increasing numbers.

For eleven months in 1982, James Dillon and two other people operated Big D Automatic, but the station had a weak signal and was never a great success. Dillon is certain that, "had the system been introduced on a very strong transmitter it would have been very, very successful...it's a pity that radio had come to that. Then what Nova were doing wasn't far from it anyway...it was automated radio...except they programmed the disc jockeys as well."

An actual decision was never made to pull the plug on Big D Automatic. Rather in late 1982 a fault developed in the transmitter, which was fixed, only to develop again. A transformer was blowing, and it would have taken over a month to have it re-wound and "that would have meant that we'd have missed the whole Christmas period." This would have resulted in not only the temporary loss of revenue, but indeed the loss of whole advertising contracts. Just before Christmas 1982 The Big D stopped transmitting, never to broadcast again. "I was glad it happened at a stage when few people were involved...and it was easy to step out of it," said Dillon, "it seemed like there was no point in staying in, it was over and that was it." Somebody else who wasn't very sad to see the end of The Big D was Eamon Cooke, "I said they'd go downhill," he confided "and if I could help them along the way, at any time, I was always willing!"

The late summer of 1982 saw ARD close down for the last time. The station had ceased to plan ahead, and as time went by it became less and less like the ARD that existed in the late seventies. Finally on September 15th the station broadcast for the last time. After the emotional closedown, the microphones were kept open on FM, and Dublin listened to the sad sound of the studios being dismantled. With the departure of ARD and The Big D, the only remaining stations from the pioneering days were Radio Dublin and Radio City. In January 1983 a fire at the City studios put the station off the air, forever.

Going into 1983 then, Radio Dublin was the only surviving station of all those who had set the ball rolling back in the sixties. But it wasn't just the stations that had ceased to broadcast, most of the pioneers had too. Both Jimmy Lynch and Eoin McDonagh (Ed McDowell) who were responsible respectively for the very early stations, Radios Melinda and Empathy, left mainstream broadcasting in the mid seventies. Ed however never got over the radio bug and could be heard popping up on obscure stations well into the eighties. After leaving ARD, Bernard Llewellyn invested heavily in Dublin advertising freesheets, but his publishing empire went to the wall in the early eighties and he has kept a low profile ever since. Big D boss James Dillon went on to establish his own successful video company in Dublin. The colourful Don Moore expanded into various areas after leaving the radio scene. He sold CBs during the 'goodbuddy' craze of the late seventies, then branched out into electric kettles, toothbrushes etc. and according to himself, various financial transactions. After splitting with his wife Debbie, Dr. Don went to live in Sutton.

With the advent of Radio 2, ARD's divine trinity parted company forever. Both Mark Storey and Declan Meehan worked a short unhappy spell for RTE before moving to the greener pastures of London, to become producers with Capital Radio. However Davitt Kelly, who started Radio Atlantis from his adolescent bedroom, never recovered from the loss of Big D Weekend. He went on briefly to operate KELO from Swords, before moving to Youghal, Co. Cork, to manage a family boutique.

As for the Radio Dublin connection? Billy Ebrill, the man who built the transmitter which put Radio Dublin (and Irish pirate radio) on the map, qualified as an engineer and then worked for the Department of Posts and Telegraphs (the irony!) before moving to the ESB. He is no longer involved in broadcasting. Other temporary guardians of Radio Dublin included Roger Lloyd and Ken Sheehan. Roger is employed by Dublin Corporation, and he still maintains an interest in broadcasting, while Ken went on to work in various professions. As for all the other pioneers, "have they like me no station in life?" asks Ken Sheehan. Apparently not.

Southside Radio and Radio Leinster both closed in mid-1983.

In June a new station started operating from Dublin, Capital Radio. Its aim was to out-Nova Nova. Broadcasting on 98 FM, the station sent out carrier beams all through June and on the twenty-seventh officially opened with Tony Allan behind the decks. Capital Radio had offices on Dublin's St. Stephen's Green and studios in Milltown, in the 'Alto Video' complex. On June 17th, a pirate television test card was broadcast around Dublin. Its location according to Eamon Cooke was the same as Capital Radio. Throughout the summer Capital struggled on. On August 4th, Sunshine Radio switched to 101 FM, in stereo. By late August Sunshine was booming out all over Dublin, as Capital Radio's broadcasts became less and less frequent, until finally they stopped altogether. Then another Cary project took to the air. On 28th September 1982, Radio Nova's sister station, KISS FM, started broadcasting on 102.7 FM. "We tried all kinds of formats on KISS FM," said Chris Cary, "very disco music...then we went to a family entertainment thing...and then we got it slower - and the slow one worked."

By November 1982, it was estimated that nearly sixty pirate radio stations were operating in Ireland. Sixty is a conservative figure as it does not take account of short-wave or minor weekend hobby operations like Radio Snowflake, Westside Radio, Concord Radio, Dun Laoghaire Local Radio, Soundout Radio, Emerald Radio, Quad and all the festival radio stations that came and went with various events. If all the minor stations were included this would put the total of unlicensed radio stations operating in the Republic of Ireland in late 1982 at nearly ninety! The situation was getting completely out of hand, and was to get worse. On 4th November 1982, the Fianna Fail government, which had only been in power since February, lost a vote of no confidence. The twenty third Dail was dissolved and yet another General Election was called, the third in only eighteen months.

As the date of the election drew closer, it became obvious that this time around RTE were laying their cards on the table. On November 5th politicians from all parties were warned that if they co-operated with unlicensed radio stations during the election, RTE would black them. They would receive no coverage on the national airwaves. The ban on "any politician or candidate" came into effect from 1am that morning. The RTE group of unions were wasting no time. A spokesman for the NUJ explained, "This decision has been taken in the light of the abject failure of politicians to legislate for the orderly development of broadcasting in Ireland. This failure has resulted in the widespread flouting of existing laws and so threatens the jobs and livelihoods of journalists in RTE and in the National and Provincial Press." The RTE body also wanted an increase in the licence fees to offset the massive losses at Montrose. As a direct result of all this pressure, instructions were given to candidates by the leaders of all the main parties not to co-operate in any way with pirate stations.

The pirates weren't long in responding to this latest ultimatum from RTE. Sunshine boss Robbie Robinson said that "the RTE unions are using us as a whipping pole to get what they want." Mike Hogan, acting Managing Director of Radio Nova, said that their election programmes would continue, "...and we will be inviting each of the political parties to send a representative." With RTE's election coverage seriously curtailed, due to lack of funds, the pirates felt that they had a real role to play. Sunshine Radio stretched its limbs and caused panic when on November 22nd, two days before the General Election, an interview with Albert Reynolds TD and Michael Keating TD was broadcast. There was uproar in the Fianna Fail camp. The next day however it became clear that the interview was an old one, a tape that Robinson had broadcast to remind people to raise the question of local radio with canvassing politicians. "I think we had three politicians here, that was all," said Eamon Cooke, "last time around there was no end of them, there were two or three a day!"

This election saw RTE and the unions therein combine in a desperate attempt to force politicians to make a stand on the subject of unlicensed radio. From RTE's point of view, the threatened blacking of politicians had been a success.

The election over, a Coalition Government took office. They had a working majority and it looked like things were, at last, going to happen.

The Power Station

By January 1983, Chris Cary was once more blowing his own trumpet. As early as April the previous year he had been boasting about a proposed 50 Kw transmitter for Radio Nova. Then in early 1983 he announced a revised plan, which mentioned once again Breakfast TV and a third station in the Nova family. This station would broadcast to Britain and the Continent. Around this time Cary supposedly entered into negotiations with Tony O'Reilly of Independent Newspapers and with the Smurfit group. The reasons for the discussions were financial, with Tony O'Reilly keeping his finger on the financial pulse of the electronic media.

By February, Cary's enthusiasm for Breakfast TV had diminished, and plans for developing this area were dropped. Around this time Ted Nealon was appointed Minister of State with responsibility for broadcasting. His job was to clean up the airwaves, introduce local radio and therefore bring to an end what RTE's Fred O'Donovan had called "the greatest scandal of recent years". With all this activity one of Ted Nealon's first announcements on pirate radio went almost unreported. On Thursday February 24th the Minister promised an early clamp-down on unlicensed radio stations. His voice was lost in the wind; the little boy had cried wolf far too often.

On 29th March 1983 KISS FM gave away £5,000, the sort of competition Radio 2 could never hope to compete with. Loving the publicity Chris Cary kept the interviews flowing, as he waffled on at great lengths about his latest toy, an export radio station, Radio Exidy. The owner of Ireland's former Butlin's holiday camp, Phelan McCloskey, was approached by Cary. Chris wanted to site his new export station in Mosney, on the east coast and broadcast into Britain. But while Chris felt that the privilege of having such a station on the holiday camp was its own reward, Mr. McCloskey wanted more concrete rewards. Cary wasn't forthcoming and the deal fell through.

Exidy initially planned to broadcast on long wave (1181 metres), using a massive 500 Kw transmitter. After the Mosney location fell through Cary planned to re-locate the station to the old Nova newsroom in Herbert Street. This time he would use a 50 Kw transmitter on medium wave. Chris Cary remembers his plans for export radio fondly. "Exidy was a wonderful plan that was to broadcast to the Brits and take lots of money from them." From the very beginning Cary planned to broadcast from Ireland into the UK; that's what he and Phil Solomon had planned for Sunshine. "Exidy is an obvious thing to do...you've been listening to their radio for the last forty years, it makes some sense to sell to them," said Chris, and sell he intended to do.

Although there had been plenty of threats and lots of hot air, previous Irish governments had been rather lenient on Cary. Things were very soon to change. Robbie Robinson hit the nail on the head when he said, "....the final straw to break the camel's back was the importation of the 50 Kw transmitter and the appearance in the British magazines of the plans for Radio Exidy."

A Bolt From The Blue

"Illegal stations are always at risk of action against them. Those who operate illegal stations should be under no illusion as to that."
Jim Mitchell T.D.
Minister for Communications in the Coalition.

"I was in bed at the time" confessed Chris Cary, "they rang me up and said, 'the P and T are going bananas in Nova,'...and I thought they were talking about telephones!" The government had in fact launched a clampdown on pirate radio stations; it was Wednesday 18th May 1983, the day of the Department's first raid in nearly five years.

The Nova Raid, May '83.

To understand the significance of the raid on Nova, one must put the pirate radio scene in 1983 into perspective. Pirate stations had been operating with little or no interference from government agencies since 1979. The stations had come out of back rooms and attics to occupy impressive buildings on busy streets. Pirate radio had become a lucrative business enterprise. In the first half of 1983 alone, 266 Irish firms had ceased trading; in a recessionary period Irish business was struggling to keep its head above water. Unlicensed commercial radio, on the other hand, although technically illegal was highly profitable. "Radio Nova is turning over a million pounds a year," said Tony Allan. "In 1983, if you're doing a turnover of a million, you can hardly term it a shaky business. It is a very sound and profitable business." Not every Irish pirate was in the same league as Nova, yet most stations which kept an eye to the needs of their market made some money, however small.

By 1983, pirate radio had fully integrated itself into the economic, political and social fabric of Irish life. It became hard to imagine a time when it didn't exist and for many people it was synonymous with local radio, as acceptable and as much a part of the community as the local newspaper. Mrs. Una Sheedy confessed that she was "deeply disappointed". Mrs. Sheedy worked for RTE.

What caused her so much angst and distress was the fact that students on an RTE Community Radio course seemed to be under the impression that if local radio was being run by a reasonably respectable body, then it wasn't illegal. "Sometimes it was quite difficult to make them realise that all local radios, other than services involving RTE, like Cork Local Radio or Mobile Community Radio, are actually illegal!"

When political parties ran stations, when stations raised money for charity, when RTE personalities did voice-overs on pirate commercials and when the government accepted PRSI and PAYE payments from the pirates, the general public could be forgiven for believing that stations were legal, and that they would continue. The raid on Radio Nova, therefore, came as a bolt from the blue.

Ted Nealon had mentioned closing stations, but then he'd mentioned a lot of things, including Independent TV. In March, on the RTE television programme *Today Tonight*, Nealon stated that the pirate stations would be banished, "in association with bringing in local radio, so that you don't leave a vacuum, and create all sorts of difficulties." By April 26th Minister for Communications Jim Mitchell was contradicting Nealon, saying that while he intended to introduce legislation "to suppress these stations", in the meanwhile action would be taken under existing law. A month later stations were raided, even though on that television programme in March Ted Nealon stated that a deadline would be given before any such action. Somehow between March and May the Department had undergone a change of mind. What made Mr. Mitchell sanction the raids will not become known until the release of public records early in the next century. Even then question marks will exist over some of the details. One can speculate as to why the stations were raided; but first, what exactly happened?

The morning of May 18th was well under way at Nova. Declan Meehan had just finished his breakfast show and Tom Hardy was on air. At 9.30am a group of Gardai and officials from the Department of Posts and Telegraphs led by Detective Sergeant John Maguire, who had directed action against the stations in the seventies, arrived in Herbert Street. Tom Hardy takes up the story: "The gentlemen from the P and T...asked me to cease transmissions, which I wasn't able to do because I don't have keys to the transmitter halls...so we continued... They became a little bit impatient because I couldn't get the keys for them and eventually, because we couldn't get anyone down here with the keys, they decided that they would then go to the transmitter site in Rathfarnham. I went with them, and they proceeded to attempt to break open the cabins but eventually some of our people arrived with the keys." While the men were travelling to the transmitter site in Rathfarnham, Radio Nova played station jingle after station jingle. Eventually the Department gained access to the equipment and Nova fell silent. "They took everything," continues Tom, "even a new transmitter which wasn't even assembled. They took that as well." The new transmitter that Tom Hardy refers to was the 50Kw rig for Radio Exidy.

On the 6.30pm main evening news on RTE Radio 1, the closure of Nova was the lead story:

> Radio Nova, the illegal station based in Dublin has been closed down. A spokesman for the Department said that the action was taken because of complaints that the broadcasts were interfering with the telecommunications of the Defence Forces and rescue services as well as ambulance and fire brigade radio...In the High Court, Mr. Justice Murphy has fixed tomorrow week for the hearing of an application by Nova for an injunction which would put the station back on the air. Counsel for Nova said they intended to challenge the validity of the Wireless Telegraphy Act of 1926, under which the station was closed.

That night near panic set in around all the smaller radio pirates in the country. No-one could guess what Ted Nealon or Jim Mitchell might do next.

Robbie Robinson was shocked to hear that Nova had been raided, mainly because his station might be next. "I rang up a lot of our acquaintances and contacts," said Robbie, "and I was told that it was because of the 50 Kw transmitter, because of interference, they'd gone too far. I expressed my concern about our operation and I was assured that it was a one off job...and I thought, well, that justifies the move they've made...and...I felt pretty confident that the information I had received was correct, and that there wasn't going to be any further raids, and so I decided not to take the station off the air."

Although "still a little apprehensive", the next morning saw Robinson up bright and early and broadcasting under his alias Robbie Dale. Shortly after 9am officials from the Department called to the station in Portmarnock. Within minutes Sunshine was silent. Nova however had returned, on low power at six that morning. The Department told the press that they would pass "no comment" on the return of the pirate. In reality they were fuming and tempers flared in Lyon House.

If the raid on Nova was a defeat, then the station's return twenty-one hours later was definitely a victory. That day's broadcasting was the most professionally orchestrated and highly successful piece of rabble-rousing public-relations ever carried out in this country. Chris Cary called it, "a proper closedown", as Radio Nova announced that they were to go off the air at 6pm that day. All during that 'last day', presenter after presenter told stories, and dragged out the memories. Each D J came on air and played a favourite record, then said goodbye. Excitement rose to fever pitch. Tony Allan came on air and as if announcing the end of the world said:

"Tonight at six o'clock sees what could be the end of the most exciting period in the history of broadcasting in Ireland, when Radio Nova goes off the air. Despite the fact that the overwhelming majority of people in this country want the right to choose what station they listen to, those in power still deny that right. There are many ways you can show your support; telephone your TD at Dail Eireann. Write to your TD, remember you don't need to put a stamp on the envelope and tonight at six o'clock come to the headquarters of Radio Nova at 19 Herbert Street and show your solidarity. If you can't get to Herbert Street, then at six o'clock blow your car horn, and blow it long and hard. The answer is in your hands. Don't let us down."

As it drew closer and closer to six o'clock, the Nova farewell broadcast became more and more emotional. Herbert Street began to crawl with thousands of well-wishers, as Tony Allan took over the programme. The minutes ticked away - and still the memories. A microphone pointed into the crowd and the cheers of support and the chanting added colour to a flawless piece of nostalgia broadcasting. The theme to 'Hill Street Blues' faded in, Declan Meehan said good-bye "and thanks for the memories." The crowd faded in, then out, as Tony Allan said a simple "good-bye" and announced "The time is now six o'clock and right now we want you to blow your horns, wherever you are!" A wall of chanting, cheering and car horns filled the air. "That's the voice of Dublin telling the people who should be listening what they want to listen to!" said Cary. With that he broadcast his emotional farewell speech:

"In a few moments time Radio Nova will cease its transmissions, voluntarily. It's a great pity that so many people that have given their all to this company, fifty three of them in all, never ever let me down and did the very best they could do, and today it's a very sad thing, to say good-bye to them all. I feel sure that we'll all be back together again and all these people will be back in this building earning the wages they worked so hard for. Bye Bye."

Nova's 'proper' closedown

The Marseillaise. A chorus of 'It's Good to Be the King'. Cheers of support from the assembled crowds. A few last chants, and Radio Nova fell silent.

Mass Hysteria

On the nineteenth, the day of Nova's 'official' closedown, mass hysteria gripped stations. At 1.15pm Radio Leinster went off the air voluntarily; the station was never really to make it back from its self imposed exile. In Cork both ERI and Southcoast closed. Radio West in Mullingar ceased transmissions at midnight, as did Bray Local Broadcast. ABC Waterford too stopped broadcasting, although they claimed it was for routine maintenance and Treble TR from Walkinstown went off the air. Not one station was left on the air as far north as Donegal and as far south as Cork, as dawn broke on the twentieth. In Dublin only Radio Dublin and the smaller ABC Radio stayed on the air.

Eamon Cooke waiting for a raid

Nova had been raided on the eighteenth, Sunshine on the nineteenth. On the twentieth, Eamon Cooke felt it would be his turn. He fortified his house, barricaded in the equipment and spoke to the press. "It is little wonder so many of them take Spanish holidays, to get the Franco method of handling things!" he said, and DJ Mike Baron added that the government action "smacks of fascism." But there was to be no government action on Radio Dublin, this time at any rate.

The station closed down its channel 2 and continued on 253 metres. With the airwaves otherwise nearly empty, Radio Dublin's popularity soared. It was like Christmas 1977 all over again, except better. One by one disc jockeys from Sunshine and Nova, and some of the smaller stations, crowded into Eamon Cooke's front room in Inchicore, which contained the tiny Radio Dublin studio. Each said their piece, then left through the packed kitchen, only to be replaced by more. With a smug smile the Radio Dublin crew let the Nova people in and patted themselves on the back for outliving the Herbert Street upstart.

That night Chris Cary brought the Radio Nova crew out for a meal, "to thank them all", and everyone was wondering what to do next. It was decided to put Nova back on the air. If the station was raided, only a few hundred pounds worth of transmitter could be taken. If Nova didn't return, the station would go bust in the most spectacular manner. "We're talking two or three hundred thousand pounds of fuck up if we don't go back on," said Cary. "The balance of convenience is clearly on our side and at least we made a second attempt to come back and we got back...It was very ropey. After about five days went by, well if they're not going to raid us within five days, there could be another era coming up." So on May 21st Radio Nova returned with a smaller transmitter, and smaller expectations. No longer did Radio Nova "Broadcast from Dublin", it "Broadcast to Dublin." On the subject of Nova's return, a "top Fine Gael source" told a Dublin evening newspaper: "That's it!- Cary will get no licence from us. That's him finished!" Cary must have been quaking in his Gucci shoes.

In the region of one hundred and twenty-five thousand signatures had been collected in support of 'Independent Local Radio'. The time was right for yet another Free Radio March, which was to take place on 27th May 1983. It was organised by Radio Dublin, in co-operation with other pirate stations and the NIBO which had been given a new lease of life. The Free Radio March assembled outside the GPO and thousands of young and not so young people walked on Dail Eireann. Unfortunately somewhere along the route half of the supporters got lost, only to arrive outside the Dail thirty minutes late. There was nothing particularly striking about the speeches made at the march. Each speaker told the multitudes exactly what they wanted to hear. For example, Young Fine Gael told Mitchell to watch it as they were "out for his guts!" Speaker after speaker rejected the title 'pirate' and said they wanted to be legitimate. As the crowd roared "We want Nealon," an invitation went out to any

The Free Radio March, May 1983

politician of any party to speak to the assembly. Only Alderman Sean D. Dublin Bay Rockall Loftus took them up on their offer. Several politicians, namely Mary Harney, Mary O'Rourke, Albert Reynolds (ex-Minister for Posts and Telegraphs), Bertie Ahern (who was involved in the Fianna Fail pirate, Election Radio 1982), Terry Leyden (Fianna Fail spokesman on Communication) and Senator Donie Cassidy (heavily involved in showband promotion), stood in silent support safely within the confines of Leinster House. Had their support been more vocal, maybe something would have come of the march. As it was, Michael Tiernan presented his estimate of a quarter of a million signatures to the doorman at Leinster House. And that was it.

Pulling The Plug

Just what factors made Nealon and Mitchell pull the plug on Sunshine and Nova have been debated long into the night by those closely involved in the stations.

On 8th June 1983 Mitchell stated in the Dail that interference was being caused to various essential services. The source of that interference, he said, had been traced to various pirate operations. According to Ted Nealon among the most serious complaints came from "the North Eastern Health Board, who reported that their radio system for the accident and emergency services was rendered useless for a period of four days, from 16th to 19th April of this year...This was the case also with the Drogheda and Dundalk fire services and with the Meath fire service...A similar complaint of severe interference to the Dublin ambulance services. On receipt of the complaints my Department monitored the frequency bands. Tests established that interference was caused by a combination of signals from Radio Nova and KISS FM." Interference was also noted at Dublin airport, reportedly traced to Sunshine Radio.

Interference from pirate radio had been experienced for nearly two decades. According to the Minister for Communications, his Department raided stations thirty times between 1977 and April 1983. But raids were not consistent. During the lull, pirate radio had grown to maturity with the arrival of the super pirates. Why not strike before the great boom in the sophistication of stations? The reasons are many and include political instability, weak legislation and the threat of a public backlash. But all these elements existed in May 1983. So why were the stations raided?

The answer lies in the Chris Cary grapevine.

•••

From the day that Cary set foot in Ireland, it had been his intention to broadcast into Britain from the Republic. As far back as 1980, Chris had been boasting about his plans for export radio. Early in 1983 a 50 Kw transmitter was imported for that proposed station, Exidy. This was reported widely in British trade magazines. When Nova was raided, the Exidy transmitter was taken, one week before the station's first scheduled broadcast.

What is most likely then is that the British Government corresponded with the Irish Government on the subject of an illegal export radio station operating from Ireland. Radio Nova had already been rebroadcast in England, blocking Red Rose Radio, a licensed independent station. This interest from the UK, plus the success of Nova both at home and on the Isle of Man, coupled with the Government's dawning realisation that the embarrassing problem of national radio piracy was about to bubble over into Britain, all forced the Coalition's hand in the matter, and Nova was raided. Sunshine was most probably a political casualty.

On 11th August 1983, Ted Nealon, Minister for State with responsibility for Broadcasting, announced his Local Radio Bill. Thirty local radio stations would be established, with RTE owning a maximum of 25% in any one station. As local radio was such a contentious issue, public support would be vital for the success of government plans. The raids on Sunshine and Nova had been a huge blunder and had completely undermined the authority of the government. Therefore the Local Radio Bill would be the first piece of broadcasting legislation to be handled by an interparty committee. The Oireachtas Committee was to sift through and assess the fifty-seven various proposals made by individuals and special interest groups. This would hopefully open up the legislative process to the people and make government more democratic.

Some of the more interesting submissions came from RTE, the Irish language group Gael Linn, Eamon Cooke, Robbie Robinson, John E. Nolan's EBC, and the NACB, who believed that local radio should be built "from the grassroots up". They interestingly had the support of Muintir na Tire and the shadowy right-wing religious group, the Knights of Columbanus. Everyone had a finger in the pie, and some arguments were more reasoned than others. One submission called for the banning of all music stations as the writer could not stand the "blasting out of the drug-taking, sex-obsessed singers"! The Oireachtas Joint Committee however was not obliged to issue a report or to offer recommendations on draft legislation. It was powerless. Instead of involving the public, it, in the words of the *Magill Book of Irish Politics*, "added another sluggish layer to government."

However, the legislation had been published and the Government had a voting majority in the Dail. This time everyone felt the game was finally up –

How wrong can you be!

At the time it was not apparent to the public just how divided the Coalition parties were on the question of local radio. Minister Mitchell was in reality getting very frustrated by his lack of progress. He stated in the Dail, "I want to put on record the efforts I made in four and a half years and what I think is the absurd and totally unrepresentative behaviour of the Labour Party." In 1988, in a rare insight into the mechanics of the Coalition government, Jim Mitchell explained that neither before the publication of his Radio Bill nor during the eight months it was debated by the Joint Committee on Legislation "was there any intimation to me as Minister from any of my Labour colleagues that there was the slightest problem with the Bill, but after the Joint Committee on Legislation completed their report...the first I heard of the Labour Party's 'problems' was in the newspapers. Subsequently, amazed though I was, I tried to discuss with the Labour Party what exactly they wanted. After many meetings it was clear that that party did not know what they wanted."

10

Black Magic & The Five Deadly Sins

"The people that have come and gone in this profession have been the ripoff merchants , the cowboys who were in it for a quick buck. I'm not a cowboy and I'm not in it for a quick buck!"

Robbie Robinson, Director, Sunshine Radio.

"They took about £45,000 worth of equipment," estimated Robinson, "and my reaction was to get it back, and that's why we went for an interlocutory injunction."

After the raids both Sunshine and Nova served separate plenary summonses on the Department of Communications. Their cases came before Mr. Justice Murphy in the High Court. Here the Justice decided to hear both cases at once, while passing separate judgements. What Cary and Robinson were trying to do was double edged. Firstly they wanted their equipment returned and secondly they wanted to have the Department's action and therefore the 1926 Act declared unconstitutional. This would effectively legalise pirate radio in Ireland.

"He could have thrown that case out in an hour," explained Cary. "He could have read both affidavits, which would have taken 15 minutes. 'Well I've heard both sides. Radio Nova is illegal and that's the end of the case.' But he didn't!..he asked for more things and even when he got to the end of it all, he then listened to the Sunshine argument, which was almost identical to ours - and then he said he wanted a week to think about it!"

On the following Friday, June 10th, in a reserved judgement, Justice Murphy declined to grant an injunction to Radio Nova. He also refused Sunshine's request. In summing up the Justice said it would only be in the most extraordinary circumstances that the Courts would seek to restrain a Government Minister from carrying out a duty, clearly his responsibility under the law. He added that he could not return Sunshine's seized equipment, as this would enable the plaintiff to commit another criminal offence. "Unfortunately we got tarred with the Nova brush," said a philosophical Robinson, "we defended our case with sound evidence. Nova didn't. But...they were heard before us!" Two days after the judgement Sunshine joined Nova back on the air.

With the failure of the interlocutory injunction, the superpirates lost the first round of their battle with the State. However by October things had taken a dramatic turn. "The next part of the legal procedure was for the Department of Communications...to take me to court and to take the company to court, which they did," explained Robinson. Here Justice Wine, to the dismay of the Department, overruled the verdict of the previous court and ordered that the confiscated equipment be returned. In summing up the Justice said, "The sooner the new legislation which is proposed is introduced to legalise the operation of stations such as Nova, the better. Competition in business, just like anything else is not only good but healthy for everybody concerned. It can only give additional enjoyment and variety of programmes." With that he fined Cary £25, a week later he fined Robinson £20. He gave them both seven days in which to pay.

In the wake of this embarrassing ruling, rumours abounded that the Department of Communications had raided Nova and Sunshine without cabinet approval. While the witch hunt continued, Cary took to the stage in glory, plugged in his 50Kw transmitter and blasted Radio Nova all over these islands. As the ad revenue began to flood back into Herbert Street, Cary recalled, "We didn't expect to win and we didn't, we just won a few points, but it was a very expensive exercise - cost £10,000...Well it was a very big cheque to write. On holiday you could use ten grand!"

In the weeks following the raids on the super pirates and the protracted court hearings, press and politicians alike were regurgitating the well chewed prejudices that have always been associated with pirate radio. As far back as 1976 the five deadly sins had begun to take shape. The 1984 RTE anti-pirate press campaign served only to enforce these cliches, guaranteeing that a discussion of the issues could never take place and that the debate on local radio would never progress beyond a slanging match. Trotting out one of the deadly sins was a good way of avoiding awkward Dail questions, justifing raids or just getting a mention in the *Irish Times*. While buzz words like exploitation, interference, ad revenue, news and music piracy often reared their ugly heads, the issues at stake were seldom if ever debated.

1. Interference

The International Frequency Allocation Board (IFAB), a sub-unit of the International Telecommunications Union, based in Geneva, have responsibility for allocating broadcast frequencies globally. The purpose of this allocation system is to minimise interference, especially on the cluttered medium wave band. Therefore, by carefully controlling the availability of frequencies and the range of transmitters, wavelengths can be shared by several countries without there being interference.

What happens when a country or an individual 'adopts' a frequency then depends on how close their transmitter is to one legitimately in operation. For example Ireland is allotted the medium wave frequency of 567 metres, which in 1984 was being used by RTE Radio 1. On this wavelength the signal from the 500Kw Tullamore transmitter could easily be heard on the south coast of England. That is until the pirate station Laser 558 started broadcasting

On May 24th 1983, a *Today Tonight* TV special on unlicensed radio was cancelled by RTE Director General George Waters. According to Mr. Louis McRedmond the decision was "an editorial one." Exactly a week later, the Taoiseach Garrett Fitzgerald told a meeting of the International Federation of Journalists that: "We believe that a Free Press is essential if citizens are to be fully informed. A Free Press in our society also serves an important monitoring function because it acts as a critic of Government and a voice of public opinion. It follows that we support a free flow of information...and we subscribe to the freedom of information."

In late 1983 trainees recruited onto the AnCO (national youth training organisation) course in local radio had to give assurances that they would never work on a pirate station. A spokesperson explained that AnCO was anxious that State money should not be seen to benefit unlicensed operators!

from a ship outside the Thames estuary. Since the Laser signal around the home counties was relatively stronger than that of RTE, Radio 1 was drowned out. So even though the Irish community on the south coast should have been able to tune into that year's All-Ireland football final, they couldn't, because of a strong pirate signal. This led to the embarrassing spectacle of the Irish Government complaining to the British Government about the problem of radio piracy!

Interference is always the first complaint trundled out against the pirates, because it's notoriously hard to disprove. Having said that, a station with a 'dirty' transmitter could cause havoc on the dial, especially to the emergency services if it operated on FM. As for stations that interfered with RTE transmissions, by 1987 they were being ruthlessly hunted down by the State broadcaster. This leaves 'responsible' stations, who chose unoccupied frequencies which often had been allocated to Ireland, but were unused. Here transmissions caused the fewest problems. A poor transmitter that is badly maintained will create problems; a well maintained one will create fewer, whether it's operated by a pirate, RTE or an independent broadcasting organisation.

2. Taking Advertising From Established Media

Despite over twenty years of active pirate radio in Ireland, RTE still commanded the largest share of the advertising market. In the financial year ending September 1986, the station earned £11.3 million from radio advertising alone. With around half of RTE's total annual budget coming from this source, holding onto every contract was vitally important.

In *Business and Finance* of August 1979 (one year before the opening of Sunshine Radio), Maria O'Brien, media manager of Aubrey Fogarty Associates, explained that "very few of the spot advertisements on the pirate stations are handled by advertising agencies. Only now and again will a client request to go on one of these stations." With the arrival of the superpirates, this soon changed.

By 1987, Sunshine Radio was arguably the biggest pirate operation in the country, with an approximate annual turnover of one million pounds. Robinson estimated that around 45% of this came from local traders, people who would never advertise on the national media. However this statistic is probably slightly inflated. Across the superpirates, only about 30% of adverts came from local traders, the remaining 70% coming from agencies. A lot of these contracts were placed by large Irish companies or by multi-nationals like Masterfoods. These contracts were mostly in addition to existing contracts with RTE. For example, in 1987, while still advertising with the pirates, Masterfoods Ltd. placed almost £1,000,000 worth of advertising with RTE, and were joint sponsors of the Radio 2 Dublin City Marathon, while Cantrell and Cochrane sponsored a programme on NRG 103 while running the 'Schools Out' campaign on RTE TV.

Therefore the total advertising market expanded with the arrival of unlicensed radio. However there was competition for the existing trade between the brash stations and the very established regional press. As far back as April 1981, the Provincial Newspapers Association of Ireland (PNAI) were calling on the Minister to close unlicensed stations. The Association claimed that the pirates posed a threat to jobs in local newspapers. The PNAI President Nicholas Nally also stated that stations "are seriously challenging (the press) for the limited advertising market on which newspapers depend."

A small pirate station did not have the overheads a local paper would, yet it could quite easily eat into the available advertising pool. The worries of the PNAI were justified. With printing costs spiralling, and with VAT on newspapers, Mr.Nally felt that, "The economic circumstances which we face are so daunting that we have agreed that we cannot permit ourselves to be further fobbed off with pleas of patience while no action is taken to deal with pirate radio."

Nally and the PNAI were going to be fobbed off even further!

3. Failure to Pay Royalties

The constant diet on pirate radio was music. Some stations broadcast this extremely cheap programming 24 hours a day. However under the terms of the Copyright Act, 1963, the Performing Rights Society (PRS) is legally obliged to collect monies (between 5% - 14% of annual turnover) from stations. This money is then paid to artists in the form of royalties. In 1982 PRS payments alone cost RTE £400,000. Most pirates paid nothing. Larger stations however did pay the much smaller sums owed to both the Mechanical Copyright Protection Society (MCPS), which covers the right to mechanically reproduce records and Phonograph Performance Limited (PPL), which pays fees to the record companies.

The problem with the PRS then lay in the fact that the society could not issue a licence to an illegal station. Neither could the MCPS or PPL, but they both accepted payment from the pirates. "I wish the Government would rectify the situation as it's causing an awful lot of embarrassment," said PRS manager Pat Condon in 1982.

"You've got to pay your way," said Robinson, who along with Chris Cary and Jimmy Smith had offered to settle with the PRS (they made much of this), but their cheques were constantly if reluctantly returned.

There was a lot of money owed to the PRS and by 1984 the society found it increasingly hard to ignore the growing pressure from members to collect from the pirates. "We have waited patiently for a number of years for the Government to properly regulate community/commercial radio. It hasn't happened." With that Mr. Condon and the PRS started to collect royalties owed by the pirates. Although in reality only a tiny minority made the payments, unlicensed stations took another step towards achieving legitimacy. As stetsoned Jimmy Smith put it, "It will stop people from saying that we're parasites!"

4. Piracy of News

"We do not steal the work of journalists," wrote Robbie Robinson in a letter to the *Irish Times*. "Our news staff work hard and against great odds to provide a 24 hour news service." The larger stations employed some NUJ staff, but this alone doesn't make a news department. The source of most bulletins on pirate radio was RTE. "Fairly basic," is how Keiran Murray described the news gathering techniques used at Radio Carousel. "We monitor RTE's news, Radio Ulster, Ceefax and Teletext. So we'd take something off the Ceefax, listen to RTE news, re-write the stories...or if it had a local flavour we'd add to it." John Miller's station in Letterkenny was more indicative of the small pirate operations. "We had a guy doing local news," he explained, "but pirated a lot of stuff off BBC and RTE. That really was our main news source. Our local news was bits taken out of the the local newspapers and bits supplied by people who knew us."

Radio Nova made a point of mentioning their Press Association newswire, whenever RTE mentioned news piracy, and while Nova did have a newswire, other stations didn't. It would be foolish to claim, and many people did, that RTE, the BBC and the press weren't raided for news - of course they were. We've already seen that Eamon Cooke simply re-broadcast the RTE Radio 1 news. Journalists cost money, and it is cheaper and easier to plagiarise news, and this is what happened in all stations some of the time, and in some stations all of the time.

5. Exploitation of Workers

In the early days of the hobby pirates only the station elders got paid, even though the amounts of money to be made in radio then were tiny. With the advent of the superpirates, DJs were put on a more secure financial footing. "We paid people from day one," said Robinson, adding that in 1987 his presenters were on around £200 for a twenty hour week. This was also true of ERI in Cork, while at Boyneside Eobhain McDonnell (an ex-builder) would pay Keiran Murray and others for turning up, even if there was no work. At Q102 the big name DJs were getting considerably more than many presenters in RTE radio or television. They were also given paid holiday trips abroad. Smaller operations used voluntary staff, as did Bray Local Broadcast, the 'prototype' community radio station politicians pointed to when they felt worthy and had to say something on the subject of local radio. But behind the glossy veneer of some commercial radio pirates, there did lie ruthless exploitation. When Nova newsreader Jenny McIvor tried to negotiate a pay rise with boss Chris Cary she was given the cold shoulder. She was working a 55 hour week for £71.75. After a bitter confrontation which brought the wrath of the NUJ down on Nova for the first time, Cary upped her pay by the paltry sum of £25. As we shall see, this was only a taste of the even greater trouble that was to follow.

"It's true to say that Christopher made a considerable amount of money out of Nova," said Mike Hogan. After the 1983 raids, the *Sunday Tribune* reported that in 1981, Radio Nova's expenses included a management fee of £49,200. This was in addition to directors' salaries of £18,662. While disc jockeys on Nova were paid well and not taxed, journalists on the station had a harder time, and often had to sell adverts on commission to earn realistic wages. However, contrary to popular opinion, this type of disposable employee was not unique to the pirates. In RTE, presenters, DJs, continuity announcers, researchers and increasingly production staff found they had no contract with the station. Rather an 'on the spot', single payment would be made per unit of work i.e. a report, or shift. Casuals or freelancers like this could be let go at a moment's notice, or kept hanging on a string indefinitely. Others lucky enough to get a contract, could, after its three or six month run, be let go. Again there would be no come back, no pension, no redundancy payments. Just another uncertain period, a summer or a few months on the dole, before (hopefully) another contract materialised.

With over 250,000 unemployed, people were just glad to be working. RTE knew this, the pirates knew this and the unions were powerless. In a monopoly situation, you either worked for RTE or you didn't work. Exploitation was rife, but the pirates weren't the only guilty party.

There is also another side to this argument. Young people used the unlicensed stations as a training ground. RTE is swarming with young broadcasters who learned the hard way, by trial and error, on the pirates. This has saved the RTE training department an absolute fortune.

A Bill For All Seasons

By December 1983, Mitchell's proposed legislation on local radio seemed as far off as ever. The Bill was being drafted and re-drafted in an attempt to win support from the Labour Party, the second partner in the Coalition Government. After fourteen months of re-writing, in February 1985, Government sources stated that "Major advances have been made in resolving differences between the parties at Cabinet level." In reality though the proposed legislation was still a long way from the Labour ideal of community based stations with RTE involvement.

Confusion also existed as to how many stations there were to be. Nealon had promised thirty, but Mitchell was now saying there would be seven or eight. In a true politicism the Minister didn't feel these two statements were contradictory, rather he felt that what was technically feasible might not be economically prudent! But Ted Nealon never mentioned 'technically feasible', he mentioned thirty stations. It was clear the Government hadn't a clue what it was doing and unfortunately the situation was to get worse as the Coalition held on to power by the slimmest of majorities.

By May a draft of the proposed legislation had leaked, thereby confounding the problem. The document stated that the local stations should "contribute to the enrichment of Irish culture and the use of the Irish language as an ordinary means of communication." The Labour Party were clearly getting closer and closer to the type of programming they preferred. But there was more than an implicit assumption in the Bill that it would be up to private interests and not RTE to run the stations. This Labour did not like, and it slowed things down even more. On one occasion Mr. Mitchell had agreed a compromise Bill with the Labour Party, but when it came to a discussion in the Dail, Frank Cluskey led a Labour revolt and the draft Bill was scrapped.

It had been two years since the superpirate raids; pending legislation had become something of a running joke and Mr. Mitchell was busy sticking his finger in the dam, while saying there was no disagreement between the Coalition parties on the issue of local radio. An interim Local Radio Commission was established, its task (rather prematurely) was to decide the number and location of Mr. Mitchell's latest compromise, a "two-tier" system of community and commercial stations.

This twelve member, government appointed commission (CORA), was made up of political representatives (with predictably enough a predominance of Fine Gael and Labour members), business interests, an educational correspondent, a director of the National Youth Council (at 25 years old the youngest committee member by far), George Waters, ex-Director General of RTE, and in a token piece of forelock pulling public relations, singer Chris de Burgh. Within the confines of Mitchell's "two-tier" system, the committee had a virtual free hand in designing Ireland's local radio system. The committee met once a month, and were expected to complete their task by mid 1986.

Even though governments may suffer from rigor mortis, pirate operators don't, and in the glut of political indecision, stations once again blossomed. By January 1984, the World Radio and Television Yearbook counted (conservatively), 47 "Private Stations" operating in the Republic. There were in fact nearly seventy. At one end of the scale, smaller operators were opening weekly, while at the other, Radio Nova took in an estimated £200,000 in the run up to Christmas 1983. Even though this was the period when Nova was at its peak, Cary was getting bored. Mike Hogan, who was head of sales at Nova, estimated that

Chris went out and spent fifty thousand pounds on his latest toy, Nova TV.

Nova Television

In October, heading into the busiest part of the advertising year, Cary and his girlfriend broadcaster Sybill Fennell went missing for ten days. Cary had just split up with his wife Remy. Despite more than a week of frantic phone calls, Hogan was unable to locate them. He takes up the story, "Eventually he arrived back and said, 'Right, let's go to lunch!' So I'm flabbergasted wondering where he's been. We go down to the Henry Grattan, Sybill is there, Christopher is there...He looks me right in the eye and says, 'Right, what the fuck do you know about television!'

It was as simple as that. By early December the equipment had arrived and Mike Hogan found his bedroom, above the radio station, turned into a makeshift television studio. A sheet from his bed had been pinned to the wall to act as a cyclorama, he recalls. "Sybill was sitting in a chair, an armchair with a big plastic plant beside her. There was a domestic video camera going through a VCR machine into the link transmitter. Up to the mountain. Back out on Channel 66. And coming back in as a picture! We were in television!"

The Nova project had proved extremely successful for Cary and his 26% partner Gene Brady. They now had two radio stations, a TV station, a short lived Nova School of Broadcasting, Club Nova, and a 'boogiebus' to ferry all the teenyboppers out to Nova Park in Rathfarnham. At this time too, the Eamonn Andrews Organisation, which controlled Dublin's Gaiety Theatre, a floating restaurant, a host of nightclubs and a recording studio, had hit financial problems. Cary, seeing an opportunity to expand his empire cheaply and quickly, put

Just some of the people who started on the pirates and who went on to work for RTE :
Richard Crowley, Dave Fanning, Mark Storey, Declan Meehan, Tony Fenton, Jenny McIvor, Simon Young, John Clarke, Gerry Ryan, Marty Whelan, Andrew Hanlon, Ken Hammond, Mary Dinan, Dave Heffernan, Michael Dwyer, Emer Woodful, Ronan Collins, Michael Moloney, Stevie Bolger, Lucy Potter-Cogan, Andy Ruane, PJ Curtis, Neil O'Shea, Robbie Irwin, Hugh O'Brien, Karen Shiels, Colm Hayes, Joe Bollard, Ian Dempsey, Barry Lang, Eoin Ronayne, Jerry Wilson, Anna Chisnall, Mark Costigan, Julian Vignoles and Keiran Murray.

together a rescue package. He and Mike Hogan then met the company princi-
pals in the Green room of the Gaiety Theatre. Due to the delicate nature of the
negotiations, the Nova office wasn't informed of their whereabouts, which was
the height of bad timing as word leaked to the station that Nova TV was to be
raided the next day.

At half past two that morning , rather drunk, Cary and Hogan staggered
back into Nova. Mike remembers "The place was in uproar, everybody was up
and everybody was awake...So I said, 'Right, what are we going to do?' So
Christopher said, 'Strip the studio, do this, do that, blah, blah, blah' and he got
into bed and went to sleep!" With that Hogan and some DJs loaded most of the
expensive equipment into trucks and drove it away. Sure enough, next morning the raid party arrived and took whatever they could, only to ring back later
to ask for the rest. Cary obliged and Nova TV was no more.

Would it have been a success? Yes, considerably so...." was Hogan's opinion.
"We had available to us a big property in Nova Park. Game shows are very
inexpensive to promote. We see it now with satellite TV channels that the kids
like disco music, they like the pop videos and we would have had no union
control. It would have been phenomenally successful. But I think that the powers
that be said, 'We've seen what they've done to RTE already in radio. What in the
name of God are they going to be capable of doing with television?' So we were
closed." With the closure of Nova TV and the folding of the Eamonn Andrews
Organisation, two more of Cary's dreams were shattered. Going into 1984 he
wasn't a happy man, and things were to get an awful lot worse.

Although Cary was later to deny strenuously that he had encouraged his
staff to join the NUJ, the facts don't bear this out. Mike Hogan remembers
"Cary said, 'You must all join the NUJ. I won't have people telling my staff that
they can't be interviewed 'cos they're not NUJ. I want them all in the NUJ.' "
Following this there was a vigorous recruitment campaign led by newsreader
Jenny McIvor. It had been a decent length of time since her last encounter with
Cary over pay and conditions, and most of the Nova staff felt this was a golden
opportunity to join an elite union. Cary however was to regret his enthusiasm
for the NUJ, as RTE took it upon themselves to put the pirates out of business.

Say Goodbye!

In January RTE was given authorisation by Ted Nealon to test broadcast on
88.2 MHz and 102.7 MHz, Nova and KISS FM's respective frequencies. RTE
was also allocated the Nova medium frequency of 819 KHz and allowed to test
on the Nova/KISS link channels. By the second week of 1984, Cary had closed
KISS FM. Immediately RTE started to jam Radio Nova on both AM and FM
with a rebroadcast of Radio 2. "We were on 88.2 megahertz and they put a
transmitter on 88.2. We went to 88.5, which is allocated to Ireland, not to RTE,

and they went there too. We went to 102.7 and they followed us there," a frustrated Cary explained at the time. With the link from Herbert Street to the transmitter site in Rathfarnham also being jammed, the pirate was in trouble. Cary moved his station to Nova Park but in the middle of a heavy snow storm, the huge 50Kw transmitter started to drift up and down the medium wave band, blocking out BBC Radio Scotland. The mole in the Department warned of another raid, and with that engineer Brian Edgar turned off the transmitter and so averted certain conflict.

All during January and February RTE pursued Nova over the wavelengths. Whenever or wherever they came up, RTE pounced, jamming them with Radio 2. Advertising began to suffer and Cary, who was used to hiring and firing at will, suddenly found that he couldn't dispose of his NUJ staff without paying compensation, something he was not willing to do. There was also a personality clash between himself and three journalists, Jenny McIvor, Linda Conway and Shane McGowan, whom he considered troublemakers. The NUJ called out their members and the pickets lined up outside Nova. However Cary's girlfriend, journalist and NUJ member Sybill Fennell continued to report for work, much to the disgust of her colleagues. The union eventually withdrew her card.

RTE's 'jamming site' under construction

By March the situation was getting desperate. There was an NUJ embargo on the station, clients were switching to the as yet unjammed Sunshine, then to cap it all, the tax man presented Cary with a VAT bill for £150,000. It was the last straw and on 9th March 1984, Nova Media Services, which operated Radio Nova, went into liquidation. Cary left Dublin for London, and the following day it was announced that a new Anglo-Irish company, headed by Cary would take over the station "ensuring that Radio Nova would continue to broadcast." With Cary temporarily out of the way, RTE shifted their attention to Sunshine Radio and started to jam during the last week in March. Immediately Robinson activated his political connections in the Fianna Fail opposition party, but their questions on "this State funded vandalism" were constantly ruled out of order in the Dail. By now RTE had stopped jamming the old KISS FM frequency of 102.7 MHz, and Cary eventually chose this spot on the dial for his new Nova. By the summer RTE's jamming had ceased completely.

As the battle became increasingly emotional, Jim Mitchell admitted in the Dail on February 1st that he did not think it appropriate for RTE to jam Nova. He however promised legislation by the summer. RTE issued a statement on its 'frequency testing': "RTE is putting out test signals on certain frequencies which nobody else is entitled to use. If someone else is broadcasting on those frequencies they will experience interference. They have no grounds for complaint however, as they shouldn't be there in the first place." RTE then had taken the law into its own hands, and it was April before Mitchell finally got through to the station with the message that the control of the airwaves was a matter for government and not the State broadcaster. Shortly after this RTE ceased to jam the unlicensed stations and concentrated instead on a massive anti-pirate press campaign, 'Illegal Broadcasting - The Real Facts'. A campaign Robbie Robinson felt was "motivated by fear of competition and an obsession to maintain their monopoly." So he launched a counter campaign.

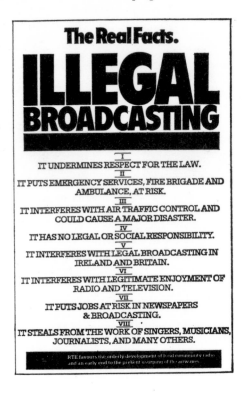

The Real Facts.

ILLEGAL BROADCASTING

I
IT UNDERMINES RESPECT FOR THE LAW.

II
IT PUTS EMERGENCY SERVICES, FIRE BRIGADE AND AMBULANCE, AT RISK.

III
IT INTERFERES WITH AIR TRAFFIC CONTROL AND COULD CAUSE A MAJOR DISASTER.

IV
IT HAS NO LEGAL OR SOCIAL RESPONSIBILITY.

V
IT INTERFERES WITH LEGAL BROADCASTING IN IRELAND AND BRITAIN.

VI
IT INTERFERES WITH LEGITIMATE ENJOYMENT OF RADIO AND TELEVISION.

VII
IT PUTS JOBS AT RISK IN NEWSPAPERS & BROADCASTING.

VIII
IT STEALS FROM THE WORK OF SINGERS, MUSICIANS, JOURNALISTS, AND MANY OTHERS.

RTE favours the orderly development of local community radio and an early end to the present usurping of the airwaves.

THE FACTS
ABOUT SUNSHINE RADIO

SUNSHINE RADIO
- is an Irish owned company registered at Dublin Castle.*
- pays V.A.T. to the Revenue Commissioners.†
- pays employers P.R.S.I.†
- staff pay P.R.S.I., and P.A.Y.E. income tax.
- has made provision for the payment of royalties to the Performing Rights Society, Mechanical Copyright Protection Society, and Phonographic Protection Ireland Ltd.
- has full planning permission for studios, radio mast, and offices.
- News is researched and gathered strictly in accordance with National Union of Journalists guidelines.
- News staff are members of the N.U.J. (Local Radio sub branch, Dublin P & PR).

SUNSHINE RADIO
- made both oral and written submissions to the Oireachtas Committee on Local Radio.
- has applied for a broadcasting licence.
- will welcome and support the introduction of Local Radio legislation.

We at Sunshine Radio believe in the concept of Independent Broadcasting,
- it would allow for more varied, flexible, and imaginative broadcasting,
- it would make available to listeners greater choice of programmes,
- it would allow easier access to broadcasting by the people,
- it would provide more career opportunities for the many talented young broadcasters in this country.

& it has been proven in recent years that this is what the people want.

* Registered in Ireland N° 78461 (1980)   † VAT & PRSI N° 4600311 V

8 - 11 Lower Baggot Street, Dublin 2
Telephone 789442 789279 789024

Robbie Robinson answered the RTE allegations
by running his own ad campaign in the press.

With RTE's jamming over Cary re-launched Nova on 102.7 FM. He was still in dispute with the union, and some of the ugliest strike incidents were about to happen.

On 27th July 1984, Cary's new nightclub, Disco Nova, was due for a high profile media launch. The union organised a picket of sixty people to parade up and down outside the Green Acres in Rathfarnham, where the disco was located. This infuriated the management of Radio Nova, and that night two picketers were knocked down when speeding cars drove through the lines of protesters. A third striker was hit in the face by a tape recorder; fortunately no one was badly hurt, but tempers were badly frayed.

Shortly after this debacle, Nova journalist Ken Hammond told in court how Chris Cary allegedly jumped from his car and threatened him while he stood alone on picket duty outside Disco Nova. According to Hammond, Cary said "Right, now I am going to mount a personal vendetta against all four of you" (Nova journalists McIvor, Conway, McGowan and Hammond). Cary allegedly then threatened Hammond with physical violence. "He put his face up against mine and said he was going to smash my face in, at the same time pounding a clenched fist into his hand." At this stage the bitter dispute had been ongoing for seven months.

As 1984 drew to a close, and business at Nova picked up, an agreement was reached with the union. The journalists were re-employed and the strike finished. The NUJ however had to return Sybill Fennell's card, and accept her back into the union. However, by June 1985 the NUJ had still to do so. Cary then contacted the union to explain that the 3 month contracts his journalists were working would not be renewed unless Fennell got her press card immediately - she did.

To the majority of listeners, this unsavoury behind-the-scenes activity was of little interest. What got them going was a £5,000 giveaway, where on hearing three discs played in a certain order, the fiftieth caller to phone the station would win the money. On 28th September 1984 those discs were played and in the resulting chaos, telephones in Dublin and much of Leinster were knocked out of action for nearly two hours. Telecom Eireann estimated that up to 80% of the 300,000 telephones in the 01 Greater Dublin area were out of order as exchanges backed up and overloaded, as thousands of people across the capital rang in to compete. Such was the measure of Nova's popularity that faults in the line were still being reported from Drogheda to Mullingar well into the night. The event had been a resounding success for the station, but a political disaster for Cary, as politicians and Telecom Eireann spokesmen lambasted him for his irresponsible attitude.

Even though the Radio Exidy project had been put on ice following the '83 raid, Cary hadn't quite given up on the idea of export radio. He still had Nova and he still had his 50Kw transmitter. Glossy rate cards were drawn up for "Radio Nova - The Voice of Europe". There were cosy photographs of "Chris Cary, Managing Director, ABC Music Radio Ltd." There were maps showing Nova's signal radiating over Ireland and the UK, where "it is also known that approximately a million people listen to the station in the North West of England alone." However Nova's sales office in Liverpool was never overworked, and "UK sales were never good." Mike Hogan admits that while the idea was sound "it's an in-built prejudice of the British population that the Paddies are incapable of doing anything right. Whilst they take a considerable amount of our good broadcasters, they still believe we're totally incompetent people!"

RADIO NOVA REPRESENTED IN IRELAND
BY TEGRAR LTD

STOCKING LANE SCHOLARSTOWN RD
RATHFARNHAM DUBLIN 16
TEL: 932167 931710

RADIO NOVA REPRESENTED IN THE U.K.
BY ABC MUSIC RADIO LTD

SUITE 411 COOPERS BUILDING
CHURCH ST LIVERPOOL L1 3AG
TEL: 051-709-9099

Nova - the sound of Europe!

But there were other more concrete problems. The Nova signal was inconsistent and inaudible to the media buyers in London. Agencies also had a dread of unlicensed radio, since to co-operate with a pirate station in the UK carries severe penalties. Also Dubliners weren't too interested in back-ups on the M62 in Manchester. These problems could have been overcome. Mike Hogan believes that Cary simply wasn't serious enough about the project, as he loquaciously put it, "you'd need to put a whole bleedin' swarm of poke into it, and nobody was interested in doing that." As the venture into the UK market was fading, Cary swallowed his pride and set up a "lost dog" radio station in Leeson Street. This was to be the home of the eight strong ABC network news team and of Magic 103.

Black Magic

"Easy listening for Dublin" is how Cary billed Magic. "He wanted a radio station that would act as his path to a licence. The idea was to set up a community radio station for Dublin with news and middle of the road music," said ex-Magic presenter Dave Johnson. However, the station was expensive to run, the advertising was low, and Cary was soon supporting the station to the tune of £2,000 a week, money which came from his own pocket. By August 1985, Cary was far from happy with the situation in Leeson Street. He was particularly worried about the daily half-hour news programme *Dublin Today*. "Leftie prisoners' rights stuff" is how Nova newsreader Dave Harvey described the show's content, while Cary felt that apart from being "claptrap", it was "dangerous and subversive" and was being recorded by the Special Branch.

This was blamed on NUJ activists Jenny McIvor, Shane McGowan and Linda Conway, who had spent 10 months on the picket line outside Nova in '84. Cary decided he had had enough and they would have to go. He contacted the NUJ to explain that their contracts would not be renewed and that he would not be offering severance pay. On September 23rd the eight NUJ employees in Nova/Magic were due to meet Cary to discuss the situation. Cary failed to show; he was in London. Sensing trouble Cary had switched Magic 103 from ABC Music Radio Ltd., to Tegar Ltd., the company that 'officially' represented Radio Nova in Ireland. However Tegar had no assets and didn't name Cary as a director, therefore it would be very difficult to legally connect him with Magic. Yet he signed all the pay cheques until the dispute began on September 25th; then they bounced.

Barry McCall of the NUJ had the unenviable job of tackling Cary on behalf of the strikers. On one occasion an agreement was verbally reached and the strike was to end. However, the next day Cary denied all knowledge of a settlement. In court, what Dave Harvey refers to as 'Cary's schizophrenia' became even more apparent. "He maintained in the Court cases that there was a distinction between Nova and Magic as they were operated by separate companies. Of course the NUJ disagreed with that". By now the picket lines outside the pirate had become a well known Dublin landmark, much to the joy of RTE who wasted no time in covering the strike for the main evening news. "We were on the picket line for six months, six very long, hard and bitter wintry months, which none of us enjoyed," remembers Dave Johnson. The NUJ organised flying pickets to Nova Park, in an attempt to embarrass Cary and his friends. The strikers carried placards calling Cary's girlfriend Sybill Fennell a scab, since as an NUJ member she should not have reported to work.

By mid-November Radio Nova was in the High Court seeking an interlocutory injunction to prevent the eight striking journalists from "picketing, watching or besetting the premises". The High Court refused their request, but the defendants promised not to call Fennell a scab anymore. According to Dave Johnson, the union "were out to find every conceivable way of pulling the station down," a tactic most of the strikers disagreed with. As one NUJ official said, "It's about time Chris Cary learned a thing or two about the power of the unions."

By mid-December the union's campaign received another boost when Mr. Justice Lardner made an order restraining Cary from operating Radio Nova from Rathfarnham without planning permission. By now those under siege in Nova Park were pouring diesel over the walls to prevent picketers sitting down.

And all this "grief" had forced station engineer Jim White and manager Mike Hogan to resign. "I disagreed with the NUJ stand," Hogan said "but I also greatly disagreed with the manner in which those people were dismissed...If they weren't going to be kept on, they were entitled to their legitimate rights and Christopher wasn't willing to entertain that, and that was wrong. That was totally wrong."

The talks and negotiations carried on throughout the winter of 1985, but both sides were firmly entrenched.

The NUJ then started to write to advertising agencies and single advertisers explaining the situation and asking for their support. Slowly this started to get results. "We lost the Irish Press Group, we lost the Independent Newspapers Group, which were the biggest single advertisers on commercial radio in Dublin," said Hogan. With these key accounts alone went £2,000 a week in revenue. "For Christopher it was a moral issue...It was crazy... we had, 'I don't give a damn if the Independent Newspaper Group never advertise with us again. I don't want them on my radio station!' That's just bad commercial planning."

The dispute dragged into 1986. Gene Brady, Cary's partner in the station, was getting nervous and threatening to call in the liquidators. Nova was getting lots of bad press and Cary had put two DJs Dave Harvey and Tony McKenzie in charge of the station. Harvey remembers "I was general manager in all but deed. I was everything in name, but I couldn't do anything. You couldn't scratch your arse without Cary's permission, and I really didn't care."

In March Cary seized all of Nova's assets. He stripped the station of all the valuable equipment and replaced it with cheap junk, which kept the station on-air. He then took his 50Kw and 1Kw transmitters and "got rid of them very quickly." Johnson continued "Everything was taken out of the station before the receiver got in." Just before they did move in on Nova a new station, Zoom 103, started testing from the old Magic premises in Leeson Street. "I remember the day Tony McKenzie pulled the plug on Nova," said Johnson, "The minute the station switched off, Zoom 103 switched on - within seconds!...Virtually everything from Nova had been switched down to Leeson Street...It was April 1986, we'd all left the picket line because we were pissed off, had enough. Nova had closed, Magic had closed - There was nothing left." Nothing that is except Zoom 103, which was later renamed NRG 103, fronted by Tony McKenzie and Sybill Fennell.

The six bitter months of the dispute left a lasting impression on the minds of those involved. Nova had gone, Magic 103 had gone, the eight journalists on strike had to look for new work, and the NUJ had blacklisted Sybill Fennell from working in Ireland and the UK. "That I think was wrong," said Mike Hogan, "I don't think it was with malicious intent that Sybill actually did pass the picket lines...I honestly don't think she knew what she was letting herself in for and if she had, she certainly wouldn't have passed the picket line. I just thought it was disgraceful to see such an incredibly talented broadcaster being shut out because of a personal relationship with the owner of a radio station that was in the throes of an argument with the union that she belonged to." Or as Dave Johnson put it: "You break an NUJ strike - Say goodbye!"

Big M Community Radio in Castleblayney with an audience on both sides of the border, has made a name for itself with fund-raising promotions for charity. Over £100,000 has been drummed up for a variety of organisations since 1983.

Sybill Fennell broadcasts during Nova's 'proper' closedown

Mike Hogan and his own personal stereo

Bees
to
Honey

"We didn't realise we were creating a Frankenstein monster in those days!"
Don Moore on the early days of pirate radio.

While the Coalition government was pussy-footing around the subject of local radio, yet another super pirate, Q102, took to the air in Dublin. This station was backed (they claimed to the tune of £500,000) by hotelier Pierre Doyle and some of his Leeson Street nightclub-owning friends. Although the station was opened by DJ Laurence John in a blaze of publicity on New Year's Day 1985, it soon hit problems when £50,000 worth of transmitter was spirited away from its hideout, up the Dublin mountains.

In the post-Christmas lull, Q102 was struggling and advertising was way down on the £500,000 that Laurence John had promised in the first year. In fact the station's expenditure was twice its income and constant injections of capital were needed to keep the sinking company afloat. "Desperate, absolutely desperate," is how Mike Hogan described the mess he had inherited. "The driftwood I'd got rid of from Nova had collected down here in Q." Over a period of two months there was quite a bit of 'lumberjacking' as Hogan and his right hand man Martin Block put the station back on the rails. By the autumn of 1985 the tight professional sound of Q102 had started to eat its way into the Dublin market.

6th January 1986 saw Dublin's new year commuters tuning into Ireland's first 'eye in the sky' traffic helicopter. Hogan himself did the traffic reports, convinced that Dubliners would like to hear a "culchie voice". They did, and the experiment was a huge success.

As Hogan's helicopter was lifting the profile of Q102 "right out of the water", his old boss Cary was floundering. His empire was in terminal decline, and both Robinson and Hogan were vying for the advertising contracts that were daily deserting Nova.

Q102's 'eye in the sky' with pilot Ciaran Haughey, his dad, C.J.,
Mike Hogan and Councillor Sean Haughey

Hot Hits

While Nova was still under the management of McKenzie and Harvey, an American by the name of Bill Cunningham approached the station with an offer. Dave Johnson remembers that Cunningham promised to make Nova "Better than it is - it'll be brilliant!" The formula he was selling was American all-music radio where "you don't need disc jockeys - they've no brains and no-one wants to listen to them!" At this stage Nova was still Dublin's favourite radio station, so it's not surprising that the American's proposals were rejected. So he went to Sunshine Radio where he and his philosophy were taken on board.

In the magazine *Sunshine Review* of September 1983, Robbie Robinson wrote: "Local radio incorporating public service broadcasting and community involvement is viable and can when well managed produce a profit." Sunshine Radio had been a model of this type of radio. With the arrival of Bill Cunningham and his 'hot hits' formula, minority programmes and community interest spots were axed, in favour of jingles and playlists.

"From a product point of view...he probably had a better quality radio station than we had," said Hogan of Robinson's Sunshine. "Before he changed format he had a nice, local, independent, family type service. He presented good quality programming...A lot of the good community aspects to the service have disappeared and I think for the worse."

Robinson of course denied this. In his opinion these public service aspects "were repackaged - they were given a facelift. You've got to understand what that 'Community' thing is." So bending the laws of semantics he explained that "we target ourselves at the 'Community' of good taste. The community of taste in Dublin." Certainly a novel definition. Robinson it would seem was suffering from a bad case of the Emperor's new clothes. "I said to him recently and he didn't even dispute it," said Hogan, "I said, 'what's wrong with *you* Robbie, is that you're upset at the fact that you sold your soul.'"

RTE, who provided students on the Degree course in Communication Studies at the NIHE Dublin with industrial placement threatened to stop doing so, because students were also going to Sunshine Radio. RTE won.

By 1984 RTE were so neurotic about the pirates, the author witnessed cars being refused entry to the RTE car park because they displayed Radio Nova stickers.

In January of 1986 Joe Jackson, manager of Nova Park unsuccessfully tried to sue Chris Cary for £5,000. This money, he claimed, was owed since May 1983, when he gave Cary a 1Kw transmitter to get Nova back on the air after the raid. Although the case was dismissed, the publicity did Cary's shaky reputation further damage.

For those left out in the cold with the closure of Nova, times were hard and work was scarce. Dave Johnson recalls that while the NUJ were very support-ive throughout the dispute, when it finished, they very quickly threatened to cut strike pay. The only work he could find though was with NRG, but there were rumours that Cary was involved.

"I met Tony McKenzie for a couple of drinks," he recalls, "and he said 'look, Cary is not involved in this radio station. He has nothing to do with it.'" Convinced, Dave went to get clearance from the NUJ. "Barry McCall said 'OK, go and work for them. If we find that Cary's involved, you're out of there.'"

Initially there were no jingles at NRG 103. But after a few months it became "NRG - The sound of Nova!" This was disconcerting as the NUJ had blacked Cary, and none of their members could work for him. Cary was also a dirty word to advertisers badly stung with the collapse of Nova. The listeners it would seem were the only ones who didn't mind the association. In that atmo-sphere, selling even the station's £99 a week bargain deal became difficult. "Agencies were saying, 'no, Cary's involved, we're not interested,'" according to Johnson, who however believed, or more likely wanted to believe, the tissue of lies being spun by McKenzie and Fennell. But soon it all became too apparent what was happening. "Sybill was talking to Chris. Tony was talking to Chris - I then knew I was working for Chris Cary...all they were interested in was main-taining the ads." This they did and soon NRG was battling it out with Q102, hot hits Sunshine, Radio 2 and a host of smaller stations for the loyalties of Dublin's listeners, and the accounts of the advertising agencies.

Promises, Promises

By November 1986, it had become obvious, even to some Ministers that it was far too late in the day to be discussing local radio. Legislation had been delayed time and again by the Labour Party's insistence on 'Community' involvement in any local radio system, and RTE, unhappy with their allotted 25% in the new regime, were lobbying for greater representation. Without firm guidelines, CORA, the interim local radio commission, was impotent. Now with a General Election pending, the likelihood of passing, or even agreeing on legislation was as remote as the Coalition's chances of holding on to power. By February a General Election had been called and Fianna Fail were in office. With the fall of the Coalition government, the community radio lobby and RTE lost a great ally, the Labour Party. With Labour influence missing from govern-ment, the end of the public service broadcasting monopoly became a distinct possibility.

Under the leadership of Charles Haughey, Ray Burke was appointed Minister for Communications and predictably enough he chose to throw out the Coalition's Local Radio Bill. But new legislation was promised, as a matter of priority, by Christmas. Although this kind of promise was as perennial as old Saint Nick himself, people in the radio world took it seriously. However it would be tough to get anything passed by Christmas, as TDs were to sit for only 65 of the 365 days in 1987!

The Numbers Game

By 1987 commercial radio in Dublin alone was worth between £2.25 and £2.5 million a year. By way of comparison, the accounting firm of Touche Ross estimate that legalised commercial radio in Dublin could be worth £2.8 million a year. In other words the superpirates were operating at almost their full market potential. There was a lot of money to be made then for the station that delivered what the advertising agencies wanted - housewives and young people with disposable income.

In April 1987 Sunshine Radio researched their popularity, convinced that with their hot hits formula they were the biggest station in the capital. To help their case they engaged in a massive press and outdoor campaign. "We've always been running promotions, promotions are part of the programming," said Robinson. But even he must have been a little surprised with the results. They showed Sunshine Radio dominating the Dublin radio market, only being beaten in three of the older demographics by RTE Radio 1."This Radio Listenership Survey was carried out in strict accordance with the guidelines...set down by the Marketing Society," ran the Wilson Research bumf. As anyone in market research will testify, there are lies, lies and damn statistics.

The research was based on how many people had listened to radio the previous day. Mike Hogan summed up the situation perfectly, "I don't think that their radio doctor, Bill Cunningham, when he did his great marketing

Ménage A Trois

On 3rd October 1986, Gardai and technicians from the Department of Communications raided the small Dublin pirate KISS FM. They did so because the station had been causing "severe interference." But in common with most other happenings in the world of pirate radio, nothing is as simple as it first appears. This raid gives us a nice insight into the eternal triangle between pirate stations, their equipment suppliers, and agents of the State.

In a letter to his customers dated October 9th, David Reddy of Telecommunications Ltd., "suppliers and installers of radio broadcasting equipment," based at Sandymount in Dublin, outlined the background to the raid on KISS FM. "The stated reason for this closure was interference to essential services, ie. fire brigade and ambulances. At the time of closure this was not accurate". The letter continues: "To outline the nature of the problem, a few technicalities have to be understood. The intermediate frequency (I.F.) of most FM receivers (including garda, fire brigade and ambulance) is 10.7 MHz...One of the cardinal rules in FM broadcasting is that two transmitters in the same geographical area must not be spaced 10.7 MHz apart." Breaking this rule leads to I.F. breakthrough or interference.

KISS FM had been operating from Dublin City Centre for two and a half years on 94.8 MHz FM. In September 1986, Boyneside Radio set up a Dublin relay on 105.5 MHz FM - 10.7 MHz away from KISS FM. The result was I.F. breakthrough. This fact was communicated to KISS by the Department of Communications on 25th September and the station closed down of its own accord immediately.

Two days following this notice KISS FM re-opened on the new frequency of 98.4 MHz FM. "Discussion with Department of Communication officials confirmed that there was no longer an interference problem." Yet on October 3rd the Department raided and confiscated all their equipment.

The letter concludes: "Let this episode be a warning to all FM transmitter operators...you could be the Department of Communication's next victim." So the game of cat and mouse continued.

A relaxed Robbie Robinson in the studios of Sunshine Radio

One of the more eccentric stations on the pirate radio scene was The Christian Community Radio run by TCG O'Mahony, "I am an officer of the court and I would not be operating the station if it was illegal." Obviously TCG had God on his side.

Before moving to FM, CCR operated on the medium wave, blocking out the signals from BBC Radios One and Two. This however didn't bother our Christian crusader who felt that "reception of BBC 1 and BBC 2 is a freak reception. So as far as I'm concerned, it is the BBC that is jamming my station." The heathen Department however raided the pirate in October 1987.

plan etc., set out to achieve anything other, and this is where his strength lay: to have people say 'Sunshine' - Mention radio, they must say 'Sunshine!"

A lot of people said 'Sunshine' as across the total 12-49 age bracket the percentages went as follows:

Sunshine 101 - 48%
Radio 1 - 44%
Q 102 - 27%
Radio 2 - 25%
NRG 103 - 20%

However accurate the research was is purely academic. What matters is that it was convincing enough to have Sunshine accepted as Dublin's most listened to radio station. Sunshine's advertising charges and the anxiety at Montrose grew accordingly. After all, all's fair in love, war and radio.

• • •

By mid 1987, RTE had again raided the pirates for talent, as Radio 2 went into 24 hour broadcasting. However the station's poor showing in both the Wilson research for Sunshine and in RTE's own JNMR survey gave management cause for concern. In the all important 15-34 age bracket, the RTE research had Radio 2 lagging behind not only Sunshine, but also Radio 1 and Q102. In fact the RTE audience research showed that Radio 2 had slipped from having a 43% share of the national market in 1980/81 to having a miserable 25% share in 1987.

After the publication of the JNMR survey, morale in Radio 2 hit an all time low. It didn't help either that a lot of the new staff who had, up to a few months previously, been on the pirate air waves every day, were often relegated to week-end slots. Staff were also anxious as the usual pre-Christmas rumours of legislation began to echo through the corridors of Montrose. "They've got an attitude problem. They don't really want to be going to work out there," said Hogan, who was right. Meanwhile Radio 2 trundled on.

Bees to Honey

"I've noticed it's usually October/November, shortly before Christmas. Headlines, particularly in the *Irish Independent* - 'Pirates To Go! Minister says Pirates to go. £10,000 fines' and all the rest. This year it'll be the same, coming up to

By the summer of 1987, RTE had adopted a new approach to pirate stations. "Where an unlicensed transmitter interferes with one of RTE's radio or TV transmitters, High Court proceedings will be initiated unless the operator ceases transmissions or moves frequency." In July Horizon Radio in Co. Kerry was successfully taken to the High Court. In August Cork station ERI closed briefly when RTE threatened legal action and in September County Sound Radio, Galway, was prosecuted in the High Court, with RTE winning the case and even expenses.

While Chris Cary and others were watering at the mouth with the thoughts of export radio, in Counties Donegal and Louth half a dozen pirates were beaming their signals northwards across the border into Northern Ireland.

By 1986 the pirates had a 14% share of the Belfast market, compared with Downtown Radio's 17% and Radio Ulster's 35%. Ian Kennedy head of BBC Radio Ulster felt that the unlicensed stations had "enough listeners to be an irritant."

On 23rd July 1987, the BBC Broadcasting Council for Northern Ireland wrote to Mr. Tom King, Secretary of State for Northern Ireland, expressing their deep concern about the pirates and saying that "the time might be ripe for some representation from the British government." By September 8th, the Department of Trade and Industry (the DTI monitor pirate activity in the UK), confirmed to the Council that the matter had already been discussed with officials from the Republic, but that they were "now following the question up more formally, by providing lists of offending stations."

By mid-October a scant and inaccurate list had been forwarded to the Department in Dublin and to the BBC Broadcasting Council in Northern Ireland. In their letter the DTI explained that the Dublin government promised "to try and assist if any of the unlicensed stations were found to be causing technical interference to licensed stations in the North." They added that legislation was at present being drafted to scuttle the Irish pirates.

Although the promise of legislation did much to placate the Broadcasting Council, Downtown Radio's John Rosborough felt that "the problem should be laid fairly and squarely at the door of the government in the Republic, which says there will be legislation at some point. But in the South, manana is too urgent a word." Even as Mr. Rosborough got all this off his chest, the National Ballroom, in Dublin's Parnell Square, was rocking to the sound of Radio Dublin's twenty first birthday party!

Christmas...but we'll soldier on into next year and say, 'Know what? Last year they said we were to go as well!' But this year maybe they will tidy something up." Words of wisdom from Eamon Cooke, spoken not in 1987, but in 1983. They were to prove prophetic.

By mid-October 1987, the *Irish Independent* was yet again promising legislation by Christmas, as Mr. Ray Burke had agreed the outline or 'heads' of his new Bill. The *Sunday Press* even went as far as promising commercial radio on air for 1st January 1988! Although the Department of Communications was denying all the rumours, by the end of October it had become clear that legislation was indeed on the way, and that its terms would be as unrestrictive as possible. On November 19th, Ray Burke published the Broadcasting and Wireless Telegraphy Bill and the Sound Broadcasting Bill. They were respectively to banish the pirates and introduce independent licensed local radio.

Mr. Burke had answered the call for licences head on, by opting for an American rather than a European radio model. Market forces, not legislation, would finally govern the number of stations in existence. In addition to local radio there would be an independent national radio station with plans for eventual independent TV. RTE would have no part in any of this. The State broadcaster had been left out in the cold.

End of Empire

For over sixty years, RTE had enjoyed the privilege and honour of being the national broadcasting service. In this role it had served Ireland well, but by the eighties, it stood alone, the last of the great public service broadcast monopolies. Commercial broadcasting had spread slowly but steadily across Europe. The Republic of Ireland, with its small population (2.5 million adults in 1986), with political and economic instability, and with consecutive governments who took a short-sighted and irresponsible attitude to broadcasting, had held on tight to the comforting apron-strings of the benign State broadcaster right to the bitter end.

The 1983 RTE Annual Report recorded an operating deficit for the year of £2,713,292. This depressing performance, unregulated pirate activity, the threat of satellite TV and a ban on recruitment, all helped to crush the spirit of RTE's staff. The Department of Communicatons commissioned the management consultants Stokes Kennedy Crowley (SKC) to conduct an in-depth study of the station. Their report was published on September 19th 1985. It found RTE to be basically sound, but over-staffed, under-productive and not cost-efficient. In addition the report recommended that, "The top management structure of RTE needs to be redeveloped to increase the involvement of senior management in the direction and control of operations and interpretation of policy to operating areas."

There was a shake-up in the top jobs at Montrose House. This saw the appointment to three new senior TV positions of Bob Collins, Joe Mulholland and Liam Miller. With these young and aggressive media professionals in charge, the atmosphere of gloom in the corridors of the TV centre gave way to one of hope. The 1986 autumn schedule saw a 20% increase in the amount of home produced programming. RTE productions dominated the top positions in the TAM ratings. Even the arrival of several satellite channels did little to dent the remarkable success that RTE TV was enjoying. By 1988 the station's share of multi-channel viewers had increased by 14%; nearly 200 staff had been shed, yet productivity was up 30%; the station was commissioning independent productions and selective recruitment had got underway.

By late 1987, even as the Minister announced his plans for the future of Irish broadcasting, RTE broke the news that it had doubled profits in a single year. The station was in the black to the tune of £6.25 million.

Although separated only by the Staff Canteen and a couple of hundred feet of grass, RTE TV and radio inhabit different worlds. While television was enjoying relative prosperity and relative calm, radio was experiencing some of the former but sadly none of the latter. The turnaround in the fortunes at the TV centre can be attributed in no small way to the leadership of Collins, Mulholland and Miller. Although their decisions were often unpopular, the end result was a vast improvement in the number and quality of television programmes. But the lack of leadership and the internal power struggles in the radio centre served only to confound the fortunes of Radios 1 and 2.

The thin green screens that physically separate RTE radio departments are nothing to the differences engendered by broadcasters' emotional attachment to their own areas. Radio 1's vast and varied schedule reflected this plurality. Programmes from Features and Current Affairs would be placed alongside those from Light Entertainment, Sport and Drama with the head of each area fighting their own corner for better programme slots, or more facilities. The controversial Activities Review Unit, set up to look into every aspect of RTE's performance, saw room for improvement in Radio 1. One of the most politically sensitive changes it recommended was the abolition of Radio 1's Light Entertainment Department. In an atmosphere of uncertainty, rumours abounded and producers at the station became deeply distressed. Early in the summer of 1987, some concerned staff members wrote a confidential report on the future of Radio 1. Entitled 'The Death of Public Service Radio', the paper was presented to the RTE Authority who refused to consider it as it was unsigned.

The report was very critical of the proposed changes in Radio 1. The loss of Light Entertainment they felt would lower programme standards. The report also warns of the threat of further centralisation of control, saying that without the protective umbrella of a departmental head, top presenters would feel alienated, as their shows could be either "dropped, chopped or sidelined". With the advent of independent radio the fears of those who wrote the report would seem even more justified. The paper concludes that unless drastic changes are made for the better, "Radio 1 will lose its dominance on the radio market. RTE will serve a fragmented and diminishing audience and public service radio will decay. In the long run we are all dead."

After much horse trading the power struggle in the radio centre settled down. Out of the ashes of Light Entertainment rose a new department, Light Music and Variety, while the head of Radio 2, Cathal McCabe, also took on the role of Controller of Music Programmes, Radio 1. While Cathal McCabe was contending with the unrest in Radio 1, his own station Radio 2 was far from trouble free. In its target market, survey after survey showed Radio 2 lagging behind not only Radio 1, but also Sunshine in the Dublin area.

Although RTE had a host of ex-pirate talent at its disposal, listeners still tuned in to the unlicensed stations. Morale among Radio 2's disc jockeys and producers (a sure indicator of a station's health) was lower than ever. When Ray Burke announced his Local Radio Bill, the number of Radio 2 people to be found sitting in Madigan's discussing the move to independent radio was frightening.

The Fianna Fail party and Charlie Haughey in particular have never been fond of aspects of RTE. The party especially dislike the 'stickie' (the Workers Party) influences they see in the station's Current Affairs and the aggressive noises that keep rumbling from the RTE group of unions. This coupled with government policy of reducing State interference in all areas ensured that RTE would be excluded from any new broadcast initiative. Minister Burke also felt that RTE had enough on its plate. The organisation operated two national radio and TV channels, Cork Local Radio, a mobile community radio unit and the Irish language Radio na Gaeltachta. On 5th November 1984, RTE launched FM3, a 'classical' opt-out from Radio 1. 1988 would bring Radio Millenium, local radio for the duration of Dublin's 1,000th birthday celebrations and Radio Tara, RTE and Radio Luxemburg's joint long wave assault on the vast UK market.

The speed with which Ray Burke finally proposed to crush the broadcast monopoly can only be paralleled with the amount of free enterprise he was encouraging. There would be two radio franchises available in the lucrative Dublin market, one in Cork city and almost one per county after that. "Dependant on demand" the Minister also promised licences for stations to service towns or other small communities. While this development had been on the cards for decades, other provisions in the new Radio Bill had not: they included a national commercial radio station and a TV channel.

In November 1987 RTE management sharpened their pencils and set to work calculating the cost of the Burke Bill. The sheer size of the proposed competition was shattering; especially worrying was the independent national radio station. If those who won the franchise were to take on Radio 1, as opposed to pop station Radio 2, RTE could be in deep trouble. In 1986, Radio 1 accounted for £8.4 million of the £11.4 million made by the entire RTE radio operation. The loss of a few of the station's top presenters to a high paying rival could well cripple Radio 1. The loss of one man in particular, Gay Byrne, would cost RTE very dearly, and could account for a drastic fall in advertising sales, and therefore ad revenue.

While independent TV had often been floated as a good idea, the sheer cost of producing quality programmes for a small audience, already served by two national channels, four British stations and half a dozen satellite operations, made little commercial sense. However several experiments had successfully taken place utilising low power transmitters and cable. In early October 1987, the Irish-speaking area of Rosmuc in Co. Galway got its own colour TV station for the weekend. To coincide with the revival of Oireachtas na nGael, the pirate TV studio was established in the Rosmuc Community School Hall, while the specially built transmitter was hidden deep in the heather, well out of harms way.

The experiment was a great success and featured Irish language discussion programmes, concerts and films, courtesy of Bob Quinn. The Connemara station cost in the region of £4,000 to set up, and according to its mastermind Donncha O hEallaithe "makes nonsense of our government's claims that it would cost £10 million to even provide a Gaeltacht television service limited to two hours a night."

Ireland and Dublin in particular have one of Europe's most modern and extensive TV cable networks. Using spare channel capacity, Cablelink (owned by RTE), have already provided their customers with satellite TV from the UK, the US and the continent. But this spare capacity can also be used to 'narrowcast' home produced programmes. To coincide with the 1984 Ballyfermot Arts Week, a limited licence was issued by then Minister Jim Mitchell for a Cable TV station. Using voluntary student crews, Ballyfermot Community TV 'broadcast' to over 40,000 homes in the southwest of the capital. The experiment was a complete success and cost very little.

In 1987 Ireland's largest and most influential production company, Strongbow, applied to the Department of Communications for a licence to operate a TV channel on Dublin's cable network. However, with the publication of the Broadcasting Bills, it became apparent that Mr Burke did not want regional narrowcasting, but rather a third national TV channel. Strongbow boss and ex-RTE Controller of Programmes John Kelleher envisages a model along the lines of Channel 4, a station that commissions a lot of programming from independent producers, and is more 'market led' than RTE. Ex-RTE Authority Chairman Fred O'Donovan has also expressed an interest in gaining the independent TV franchise, but with the total pool for advertising standing at just over £30 million in 1987, any independent TV operation is going to have to fight RTE TV. As David Holden the station's Director of Public Affairs puts it, "We will give any independent a very, very difficult time indeed."

Ducks to Water

Around the country stations were dusting off their dictionaries and buying in vast amounts of white paper on which to argue their case and apply for a local radio licence. Sally Reynolds, who represented the NACB, went walkabout selling the ideals of Community Radio. Some disc jockeys like Paul Vincent felt the time was right to go it alone, get experience and apply for a franchise. He set up Southside FM, a station which quickly gained ground in

Dublin's bay area. More established figureheads like Robbie Robinson and Pierre Doyle put the finishing touches to their financial packages, while the country's press both national and regional found that they too were entitled to run stations. This came to many as a shock, as in most countries the press are expressly forbidden from having an interest in broadcasting.

The *Cork Examiner* admitted that it was holding talks with local pirate station ERI in November 1987. Their aim was to make a joint application for a broadcast licence. While young Joe O'Connor felt it would be "a most exciting union", a Dublin magazine raised doubts about the financial history of the powerful O'Connor family.

Progress Engineering Works, owned by Joe's parents went into liquidation, owing the revenue commissioners £820,000, on 11th September 1985. The following day a new company, Progress Engineering Company Limited, started trading. According to *Phoenix* magazine "all the old company's assets were purported to be transferred to the new company, while all the old company's liabilities remained in the old company." In addition to this the liquidator found that "substantial payments had been made by the old company in respect of loans, wages, hotel bills, equipment and leasing charges on behalf of ERI." (A Companies Bill to stop cowboy directors from closing companies which have debts and opening business the following day under a new name, had been on the statute book and was promised for years. Like the promised Radio Bill however, it was constantly delayed by political stagnation.)

But this dubious publicity did little to dampen the O'Connor family's enthusiasm for local radio, or for the crock of gold Joe O'Connor saw at the end of the Cork franchise rainbow, as he admitted on RTE television: "Yes, our objective will be to make money."

Even with all this activity taking place, it didn't take long for word to spread. *The man* was back in town.

•••

After several days of test tone, at midnight November 9th 1987 a new station opened in Dublin on 100 FM. Playing non-stop music from a CD carousel, the new station broadcast anonymously until the following Wednesday.

By then however Dublin was buzzing with so many rumours about the identity of the new station, its location, its aims etc., that many had begun to suspect the handiwork of Chris Cary. It therefore came as no great shock when the pirate announced itself as the "New Radio Nova". Exactly one week after this first announcement, at 1pm on November 25th, 1987, the NRG 103 lunchtime news, which had been renamed 'Independent Radio News', opened with the following: "Good Afternoon - NRG 103 and the new Radio Nova have amalgamated in view of the pending legislation on independent radio for Ireland as announced by the Minister for Communications, Ray Burke, last week. The station name as from now is 'Nova Power 103 FM."

In an attempt to broadcast under the conditions specified in the new bill, Nova Power 103 promised news roundups on the half hour and a new hour long version of *Dublin Today*, to be hosted by Fennell, Tina Gates and Bob Gallicoe, who had recently deserted Q102. As for Cary, he was credited with being a 'consultant'.

By December the new hybrid had hit problems in the shape of one of those all too familiar interlocutory injunctions. The receiver of Nova Media Services Ltd., Pearse Farrell, felt he had to protect the good will associated with the name 'Nova'. The receiver was also concerned about some of the activities of the now bust company and with licences on the horizon he had no intention of letting Cary trade under the valuable Nova banner.

With Cary and company banned from using the name 'Nova', 'Nova Power 103' became 'Power 103'. Then it was rechristened 'NRG Power 103'. All this confusion led one Q102 disc jockey to comment that 'Q' was "the station with only one name!"

The arrival of December's long dark winter evenings, lit only by flashing fairy lights, heralded the Christmas recess and prevented the Dail from proceeding any further with the Burke Bills. The New Year saw Dublin standing proud. The capital was all set for its millennium celebrations. A thousand years of history in a city that boasted more FM stations than any other in Europe, all struggling for survival in a most competitive market, a market set for even more growth in 1988.

The Second Stage

As the radio debate inside and outside Leinster House began to warm up, it became apparent that the question of awarding radio licences to ex-pirates was going to be a contentious issue.

The *Irish Times,* not noted for sensationalism, wrote in an Editorial: "To grant a licence to a pirate station would be tantamount to rewarding it for years of consistent law breaking. This could be seen by others as an encouragement to break the law in future". *The Bray People* went even further, saying that the argument in favour of the pirates getting a licence was "about as reasoned and logical as saying that the way to eliminate illicit distilling....is to legalise poteen......or to take it to its extreme dimension, that the Provos should be absorbed into the Defence Forces to halt the carnage and murder in Northern Ireland."

These platitudes became quite common and were given a lot of air-time by RTE, and argued by many ill-informed politician. Many of them failed to see that as elected Dail representatives, it was *their* responsibility to update the law, and since they had not, they had failed the public with a grossly irresponsible attitude. As Minister Burke rightly pointed out in the Dail: "It is an indictment of the legislative process that we have for so long failed to respond to a demand we all know exists among the public for evolution in our radio services and that we have in effect tolerated a situation of lawlessness in the airwaves for over ten years."

Should the public then be blamed for mistrusting a law drafted shortly after the invention of Wireless Telegraphy and which still controlled the broadcasting need of a nation in the era of information technology? Especially as consecutive governments seemed unwilling to tackle the question of pirate radio, again to quote Ray Burke: "Part of the reason the pirate stations have been able to flourish is that we have had to rely upon the Wireless Telegraphy Act, 1926. While that Act was an extremely far-seeing Act....I am afraid its drafters did not quite see all the problems we would be faced with some sixty years down the line". This has to be the understatement of the decade.

• • •

When the Dail resumed after the Christmas recess, the Sound Broadcasting Bill and the Broadacsting and Wireless Telegraphy Bill were quickly scheduled for debate. As with the 1988 budget, both the sitting Fianna Fail government and the main opposition party Fine Gael sided together, with the Labour Party and some left wing independents firmly opposing the Burke Bills. This state of affairs led Michael D. Higgins of the Labour Party to mournfully complain that "we have the extraordinary situation where.....there will be no effective opposition".

After years of petty party politics, the two centre-right parties, Fianna Fail and Fine Gael, agreed that the country needed to be taken in hand. The Taoiseach Charles J. Haughey wanted firm government, but he needed support to ensure his minority government stayed in power, thus sparing the country from yet another election and the possibility of still another hung Dail. On a more personal level, Haughey was anxious that the confusion in the airwaves was stopped, than an independent media alternative was launched, and that he be remembered as the man who saved not only Ireland's finances but also its airwaves from chaos.

The opposition Fine Gael apparently had no problems with this; thus on 10th February 1988, the Sound Broadcasting Bill, 1987, safely passed its second stage in the Dail, by a very comfortable majority of 81 *For* and only 15 *Against*.

RTE and the Bill

"I certainly don't welcome the new competition, but we'll have to live with it," said RTE Authority Chairman Jim Culliton. "We have the professionals to withstand this new competition, provided we are allowed to compete on a level playing pitch." In order to compete with the new stations, RTE wanted equality. The RTE Cork Local Radio service, they felt, should have its broadcast hours extended beyond the existing three and a half hours a day. The ban on radio advertising between 7pm and 10pm should be lifted and the Minister should respond more promptly to requests from RTE (permission to launch Radio 2 had taken over two years to negotiate).

However the RTE wish for "a level playing pitch" would have a knock on effect on independent radio. If for instance the Cork service was to get extended broadcasting hours, there would be less advertising for an independent. The Minister was dealing with a very delicate balance. Ray Burke's predecessor Jim Mitchell recognised this, and commissioned a £42,000 confidential report on the viability of independent radio in Ireland. In February 1986 the accounting firm of Touche Ross presented their report to the Department. However this study, the only one of its kind ever conducted in Ireland, was kept under lock and key, safe from the public. This was unforgivable as the report was both accurate and thoughtful and had a substantial effect on the drafting of the Burke Bill, and therefore on the whole future of broadcasting in the Republic.

Touche Ross estimated that the annual advertising market available to independent radio in Ireland to be worth between £4.75 million and £6 million. Most of this cash would be concentrated in the larger conurbations, the report continues: "Outside Dublin, Cork, Limerick and Waterford investment in independent local radio stations would be a high risk venture and is unlikely to be profitable." The radio stations Touche Ross based this assumption on were much larger and more complex than those envisaged by Ray Burke, who firmly believes that some operations "are going to go to the wall. I don't think that it will be viable for all of the twenty four...I believe it's a matter of market forces."

At the best of times market forces are volatile. In 1985 two of Britain's independent local radio (ILR) stations closed, while another dozen were either trading at a loss or making meagre profits. But 1987 proved to be a bumper year, with revenue increasing by 27% as many advertisers switched from expensive TV campaigns to local radio.

In 1973 commercial radio was launched in the UK, and proved less successful than was expected. The reasons are many and include the very structure of local broadcasting in the UK. Nick Higham of *Broadcast* magazine called ILR "a curious British compromise". Speaking on the RTE *Today Tonight* programme he added "We don't have commercial radio on the American model or the Australian. We have attempted to impose public service broadcasting on commercial radio. That makes it very expensive...I would say to the Irish, don't do it the way we did it in England, because if you do, you will lose a great deal of money."

That imposed 'social responsibility' however was to be part of Ireland's new radio regime. As Mr. Burke said on that same programme: "This is going to be public service broadcasting in private ownership and in community ownership." The Sound Broadcasting Bill lays down those expensive 'minimum' rules. If, for example a station broadcasts for more than twelve hours a day, then "two hours of transmission time between 07.00 hours and 19.00 hours", would have to be "devoted to the transmission of news and current affairs." Other stations would have to devote at least 20% of transmission time to such broadcasts.

It is ironic that exactly two months to the day after the publication of the Burke Bills, the UK government announced plans to re-vamp its airwaves. One of Douglas Hurd's proposed changes would put an end to imposed public service elements on local radio stations. Douglas Hurd was planning for the twenty first century. He was breaking the old ILR mould, while Ray Burke was trying to stick it back together again.

The new British model sees local radio being complimented by hundreds of low power community/ethnic stations, while at least three national radio channels would be sold off to the highest bidder. This could have serious side effects for RTE.

When Mr. Hurd made his announcement, Radio Tara, the £5 million RTE/Radio Luxemburg export station, was only months from its proposed launch. Tara was to broadcast on long wave into the UK, cashing in on the absence of a British national commercial station. RTE with a 51% share in the project hoped to see £3 million a year in profits - money the station might need as Irish commercial radio bit into its native market. Now with around three UK commercial channels planned, all on the more accessible medium wave, the Tara project looked less appealing. Whatever the future held for RTE, it would certainly be eventful. As to the fearless pirates, Eamon Cooke promises to remain in the radio business, even if he doesn't get a license. "If necessary, I'd broadcast from up a tree", Eamon said when we last spoke to him.

Déjà Vu

In 1978, in Dublin's Dandelion Market, adolescent Dubliners got to know the meaning of the word cosmopolitan. In a drab grey city that as yet had no American burger restaurants, no established rock or What's On magazine, and no Leeson Street Night Clubs, 'The Dando' glowed and throbbed with weekend excitement. Here you could get alternative magazines like *In Dublin* or *Scene* which later became *Hot Press*. Here young Dublin rock bands practiced along

Eamon Cooke up a tree

side-stalls selling broken Victorian china; leather underwear had yet to hit Catholic Ireland.

Then from the stalls, frimly secured with shoe laces, hung transistor radios - hundreds of them, all blaring out Radio Dublin. Now, the Dandelion is no more. Demoslished it will soon give way to a sleazy new Shopping Mall.

Now, on weekend afternoons the lifts at London's Camden Town tube station pour thousands of squinting people out of the stuffy darkness and into the equally stuffy melting pot of Camden Lock.

In the riot of colour and languages, the divisions between the races, religions and sexes are lost. Musicians play, bag snatchers snatch, shoppers shop and hawkers sell. And what an atmosphere! Here, from the stalls that cling to the bank of the clogged Camden canals, you can buy anything from broken Victorian china to leather underwear.

From the ghettoblasters firmly secured with bicycle chains you can hear any one of the thirty or so ethnic community pirate stations broadcasting in London. Sitting in a coffee shop you will hear stories of raids by the Department of Trade and Industry, of transmitters being hidden in pigeon coops and of greatly exaggerated feats of bravery executed on the roofs of high rise council flats by renegade pirate DJs.

The feeling of déjà vu is incredible. But then it has all happened before. Nothing really changes. I close my eyes and substitute Dublin accents for those heard over the stereos in Camden Lock . I could be standing by the Green in my favourite flares, listening to the exciting sound of pirate radio while pondering a pint in Rice's pub.

12

Twenty
Years
Ago
Today......

"....*Sergeant Pepper taught the band to play...*"
from a Beatles' song

"*For too long [our] culture has been defended only through spiritual means, though it has been attacked by material arms. Being itself not only something ethereal and spiritual, but also and above all, material, it should be defended with material arms .*"
Bertolt Brecht, July 1937

With the development of mass communication technologies, we have become a people obsessed with consuming vast amounts of media. Both the technology and its subject matter have become a commodity fetish and while consumers have had an ever expanding range of hardware to play with, too often the parameters of content have been subject to a strict political and commercial control. The history of human communication, of which *The Story of the Irish Pirates* is but a small episode, is intricately tied up to the individual and collective struggle of individuals, first against nature, then by and between tribes, clans, castes, sexes, races - and much later nations and classes. In all this history of struggle, the role of communication has always been central. The major reason for this is that communication is nothing more, nor nothing less, than *the articulation of social relations between people.* How people communicate, where and when they communicate, with whom they communicate, and even to a certain extent *why* and *what* they communicate, is a function of the historical process. Like the outlaws of the wild-west, present-day pirates are not so much spaced-out 'free' individuals but real people, fighting for change, for control, for power, for communication. Which brings us to the State.

In the debate between *public service* and *commercial* broadcasting, the perspective outlined above must be kept firmly in mind. All positions in this context must be reviewed in two respects: *first,* we must take account of the origin and function of the commercial broadcasters and their offensive against public broadcasting; *second,* and perhaps more important, we must take account of the highly complicated relationship between a *public authority* , like RTE, and State / Corporate political and economic interests.

•••

It seems that two pitfalls beckon us at this juncture:

On the right, there is the risk that we get taken in by the fact that commercial radio never calls itself commercial, let alone capitalist. It uses public-relation type descriptions like *free* and *independent* and often contrasts itself to *monopoly/State* control. This is, of course, pure rhetoric which dissolves when we look at the character of most of the Irish 'pirates' or indeed the large American broadcasting corporations or the British programme companies. In different ways, almost all of these are **conglomerates of established capital interests.** Their essential function is the generation of private profit for their owners' investment. By contrast the public-service institutions are in effect non-profit making, so that revenue is devoted almost wholly to production and development of the service.

Up to this point the contrast holds and needs to be emphasised. However censorship, for example, be it imposed from above or in self-generating forms, operates, and in a sense unites, State and Commercial broadcasting in Ireland. On one side the public and those working in broadcasting campaign against Section 31, while on the other unlicensed stations have fired people for *talking too much.,* or for *planning* an interview with members of Sinn Fein.

On the other side of the argument a 'leftist' or liberal rhetoric can be equally confusing for there is no direct correspondence in a capitalist society between the State and the public interest - not in its broadest sense. In societies such as Ireland of the 1980s and 90s competitive and privatised versions of *the public interest* are at work and, as such, the State and its authorities cannot be said to represent the entire warring chess board - all the white as well as black pieces, let alone the interests of the bishops, rooks, Kings and Queens as opposed to the pawns. In monolithic societies like Khomeini's Iran, South Africa, Pinochet's Chile etc. or authoritarian societies like those in Eastern Europe, the media and access to the airwaves is strictly controlled by the State. In the west, we look on ourselves as part of the *free world* - but as we scream towards the 21st century, the old one-dimensional identification of the State with public interest has become highly questionable. We are in an era where market forces control the media and the access to the airwaves.

The debate over who has the right to control broadcasting and in whose hands should the power to make decisions lie, is no more settled now than it was in Marconi's day. We hope this book will be widely read and used to inform the debate surrounding the future of Ireland's broadcasting systems.

Postscript Static

The world of pirate radio is a world of constant change, yet the events of 11th March 1988 took the radio world by complete surprise. That Friday, the staff of NRG 103 were told the station was to close immediately.

At 6.00pm that evening, NRG 103 broadcast its last news bulletin, while behind the scenes, frantic efforts were being made to sell the station. At 9.00pm, Q102's Mike Hogan agreed to purchase most of NRG's equipment and transmitters. With that, the station closed.

"We felt it would be opportune for Q to establish local dominance in the Dublin market," said Hogan, who by 11.00pm had started to broadcast Q on his new equipment. This included a 10 Kw transmitter and four FM frequencies ranging from 99.9 to 103 which effectively surrounded and boxed in Sunshine Radio.

The almost instant demise of NRG came as a complete surprise. While there had been rumours that Q102 was winding up, Cary's renewed interest in Ireland seemed to have secured NRG's future. Now it looks as if the situation has been completely reversed. In a matter of hours, the face of pirate radio in Dublin has changed in a dramatic fashion. It appears that, as in the past, the man pulling the strings is Cary.

On 12th January 1988 Sybill Fennell and Cary had a baby boy, Nicholas. This affected the amount of time Sybill could spend running NRG103. At the same time, Tony McKenzie, her partner in NRG, had become involved in Cary's latest project. Utilising spare satellite channel capacity, Cary was experimenting with beaming radio to Europe's extensive cable network from his home in Camberley, Surrey. The results looked lucrative and far more promising than the shaky potential of a radio license in Ireland. It seems that the decision to abandon NRG was made on these grounds.

Cary reappeared in Ireland when legislation seemed on the way. In March, following the sloth-like progress of the Burke Bills through the Dail, he seems to have disengaged one more time.

The organised chaos of Irish broadcasting continues. Time will tell whether the Burke Bills, if and when they become law, will stabilise the industry or merely provide the starting point for a sequel.

38, Clarendon Street,
Dublin 2, Ireland.
Tel: (01) 794793

The newest, brightest, hottest
publishing house in town
is proud(est) to present
RADIO RADIO

Our other titles include:

Inside an English Jail
by Raymond McLaughlin (£4.25)

Sin Embargo
by J.Ardle Mc Ardle (£9.95p/b, £13.95h/b)

Vegetarian Dublin
by Carol and Brian Walker (£2.50)

Notions
by the Kilbarrack Writers Group(£3.25)

Appendix I:

The Political Parties

In March of 1988 the major political parties were invited to send a summary of their current positions on radio broadcasting to Borderline Publications.

The following is an edited selection from their responses.

Fianna Fail

Ray Burke TD, Minister for Energy and Communications, Statement of 20th November 1987:

"I wish to state in no uncertain terms that the days of illegal broadcasting are numbered.

"...the penalties for [operation, supply, advertisement, possession, use, etc. of unlicensed equipment and/or transmissions] will rise to £800 maximum on summary conviction and £20,000 maximum plus forfeiture of equipment for conviction on indictment. ...

"We are no longer in a situation where the State needs to lay down in detail what the public can have in its radio broadcasting services or where unduly elaborate or costly structures need to be established to provide or regulate these services... The task of the State [is] that of creating the environment which would allow the talent, capability and investment potential in society to gain legitimate entry into the broadcasting sphere, to see how new dynamic broadcasting services emerge and to allow society to benefit from these new services and from the gainful employment and economic activity which they can generate. ...

"The new services to a large extent will be self-regulatory. Their sole source of income will be from advertising, which will only be available if they have a substantial audience. Their audience will be their controlling factor. ...

"In relation to the question of applications from existing Pirates, the situation is that in line with the position adopted by all previous Governments they are not debarred from applying. There is, however, no question of any guarantee that they will be given licences. On the contrary, it will be noted in the criteria laid down in Section 3 [of the Sound Broadcasting Bill] that the character of the applicant must be taken into account in selecting licencees and, in this regard, pirate operators will clearly not be in line for any bonus marks."

Fine Gael

Richard Bruton TD, in a party press release dated 9th February 1988.

"The purpose of the Sound Broadcasting Bill should be to produce diversity of listening that provides a good standard of entertainment and information. There is a real danger that the Minister's legislation will achieve neither diversity nor good standards.

"He is proposing a structure where there will be virtually no monitoring of broadcasting standards. Stations may start out with very attractive programming to win the franchise, but need never again attain these aspirations.

"Broadcasting driven by advertising alone is highly unlikely to produce the desired diversity, particularly if the Minister presses ahead with local monopolies for each county. What is likely to emerge is a large number of very similar stations. There is a real need for specialized stations serving wider regions.

"The Minister says that a good Independent Authority given the remit to develop radio, would be too expensive. However, independent consultants have shown that an independent authority *could be* financed within the £180,000 the Minister intends to raise in licence fees.

"A very worrying feature of this Bill is the Minister's decision to put into his own hands power to investigate the affairs of any station and to suspend their licence as he sees fit. It is most improper that any politician should be able to hold such a sword over any section of the media. It would be unthinkable if such a power was given over newspapers. It is potentially even worse to have this power over radio."

Labour Party

News release dated 4th April 1984.

"The Labour Party has declared its opposition to the private ownership of local radio stations. The Party spokesperson on communications policy, Mr. Toddy O'Sullivan, TD said that the Party had given the matter detailed consideration over a protracted period and had canvassed a broad spectrum of opinion on it.

Many responsible people, both young and old, were concerned that local radio networks controlled by private interests would rapidly sink to the lowest common denominator consistent with achieving advertising revenue and profits. The real communications needs at community level - which were the original motivation for the establishment of the local radio network - would not be met in these circumstances.

"Communities in themselves were the best arbiters of their own needs in this regard, Mr. O'Sullivan said. They should have a major say in the broadcast content of local stations and the Labour Party will encourage the formation of broadly based community groups to exercise editorial control; control of plant, equipment and premises would remain in public ownership.

"Properly constituted groups representative of different ages and local interests would ensure that these stations would meet the widest possible range of local aspirations.

"There was a particular demand for alternative programming for young audiences and this should be reflected in the composition of each group, said Mr. O'Sullivan.

"Indeed, the Party's policy on this issue reflected particular concern for the requirements of young people. For the first time, local radio would offer them the opportunity of a meaningful and effective platform for their views and aspirations. The current lack of such a forum was a major source of contention among the young and it would be shameful, said Mr. O'Sullivan, if the unique opportunity to correct the situation now being presented were to be lost.

"Finally, the development and provision of all talents in the Irish music industry needs to be taken account of in any community local radio legislation."

Progressive Democrats

Pat O'Malley TD, speech at PD's Second National Conference, 10th October 1987.

"...this party favours an open policy with minimum State Controls. ...

"RTE would continue as the Country's primary national broadcasting service, fulfilling its public service broadcasting role but a new private sector structure must be developed to facilitate competition and to provide a choice of service for the listening and viewing public and these independent services would operate under licence from a new Independent Broadcasting Commission. ...

"We favour a two-tier structure for legal local radio. The upper-tier would comprise of local stations which would be professionally run, fully commercial stations serving economically viable catchment areas.

"These stations should be required to have a certain content of public service broadcasting in their programming and not just provide 'wall-to-wall' pop music which is typical of many of the illegal commercial stations currently in operation.

"The second-tier - the community tier would enable local communities provide the kind of services best suited to their own local needs through to having unlimited access to an airwave frequency in their area.

"These very small stations would be owned, managed and controlled by representative community based groups or persons.

"RTE should be allowed tender for a licence to operate commercial local radio stations, on an equal basis with other private broadcasting companies."

Workers Party

Proinsias De Rossa TD, in Dail debate on Second Stage of Sound Broadcasting Bill, 10th February 1988.

"It is significant that in the two Bills [including as well the Broadcasting and Wireless Telegraphy Bill] there is no indication of what attitude will be taken to those who have flouted the law over the last ten years. Various excuses have been made by spokespersons of the conservative parties for those who have flouted the law; they said they had been forced into it. I do not know of any person coming before our courts who has managed to successfully plead that they were forced to break the law and, as a result, were not penalised by a judge and jury.

...

"We believe that if we are to have commercial radio it is essential that there should be a proper Authority to set and monitor standards. ...

"The Authority, rather than the licensees, should own and ultimately control the transmitters which will be used. Private ownership of transmission equipment would be bound to confer an unfair advantage when licences come up for renewal. ...

"In relation to community radio, it is unfortunate that there is no specific reference in the Bill to the establishment of community radio stations. The initial demand for local radio came from communities who felt there was a need for them and a gap to be filled. We will be putting forward amendments to fill that gap. It is amazing that there has not been any provision by the Minister to specifically exclude those involved in the running of pirate radio stations from qualifying for licences for the new commercial stations. The fact that successive Governments failed to ensure that the law in relation to illegal broadcasting was observed has brought our legal system into disrepute. Are we now going to compound this by allowing those who thumb their noses at the law, and make large amounts of money in the process, to be free to qualify for licences for the new stations on the same basis as those who scrupulously observe the law? ...

"At present RTE have a policy of playing a minimum percentage of Irish produced records. That has been important for the development of an indigenous music industry which is now the most significant sector of the broader entertainment industry. Pirate radio stations have generally shown no such commitment to Irish produced products and I wonder if it would not be reasonable to ensure that RTE and the commercial stations have similar obligations in this area. The points I have raised are arguments for the establishment of an Independent Authority. Without it the Bill is not satisfactory and, in my view, is positively dangerous."

THE RADIO CAROUSEL NETWORK

The longest running provincial station (launched 19th May 1978)

...*FIRST* station to go stereo (1980)
...*FIRST* station to have a £10,000 giveaway (May 1982)
...*FIRST* station to have an audience survey commissioned revealing an audience of 178,000 (Landsdowne Marketing Surveys)
...*FIRST* station to win a major award, Hugh Hardy winning Radio Personality of the Year (Entertainment News February 1981)
...*FIRST* station to have a satellite (Radio Carousel, Navan 1982)
...*FIRST* station to raise £100,000 for charity (including £31,000 for Kampuchian refugees and £56,000 for Louth County Hospital)
...*FIRST* station to get recognition from semi-state bodies for co-ordinating their emergency services (Blizzard Feb 1982)
...*FIRST* station to do a live sporting commentary (Louth S.F.C. Final)

A few of the many Firsts from the station that pioneered Local broadcasting in the last 10 years.

THE RADIO CAROUSEL NETWORK

Radio Carousel Dundalk, Fairways Hotel 042 38210
Radio Carousel Navan, 28 Watergate Street 046 28762
Radio Carousel Drogheda, Boyne Valley Hotel 041 31396
Radio Carousel N. Ireland, Jonesboro, Co. Armagh
Dublin Office: 76 Dame Street, Dublin 01 325752

Appendix II:

The Stations

"No matter where you go in the country - tiny little places, big, small, in between - they all seem to have a little radio station. "
Eamon Cooke

Alternative Broadcasting Channel, Dublin
1385 AM
Atlantic Radio Galway
1978 AM
Arklow Community Radio
339 MW
Alternative Broadcasting Cork
Alternative Radio Cork
1289 AM
Alternative Radio Dublin
257 MW
ABC Radio Waterford
1026 AM
Athlone Local Radio
102.5 FM
ABC Radio Dublin
1251 AM
AMS
98.6 FM

Big D
273 MW
Big L (Limerick)
1564 AM
Big M (Mullingar)
1422 AM
Bray Community Radio
Bray Local Broadcast
97.8 FM Boyneside Radio
1323 AM
Breffni Community Radio
1170 AM
From Kilnaleck Co. Cavan
Big K (Tralee)
102.5 FM
Blanchardstown Community Radio

Big M Community Radio
99/105 FM
Boyneside 244
97.8/101.25 FM
Ballymun Community Radio
89.5 FM
Broadcast on FM only in 1987
Big K

Capitol Radio Dublin
226 MW
Capitol Radio Limerick
270 MW
Castle Radio
326 MW
Cara 9595.5 FM
Cork Broadcasting Company (CBC)
Cork Community Radio
Clonmel Broadcasting Company
828 AM
Community Radio Wexford
87.8/101.4 FM
Cork City Local Radio
1143 AM
Community Radio Youghal
99.2 FM
CBC Clonmel/Radio Carrick
1512 AM
Community Radio Fingal
105.85 FM
Community Radio Drogheda
1305 AM
Capital Radio Cork
1312 AM
Castlebar Community Radio
Concorde Radio Dublin

CNCR Radio Clondalkin
Clondalkin Community Radio
Cavan Community Radio
819 AM
CC Radio
90.2 FM
Capital Radio
98.5 FM
Community Radio Wexford
87.5 FM
CCR Limerick
99.6 FM
Crystal City Sound, Waterford
Cavan Community Radio
98.1 FM
Clonmel Community Radio
99.1 FM
Castleknock Local Radio
Carrick Local Radio
County Sound Radio
Central Radio
104.1 FM
Carlow Community Radio
1044 AM
Centre Radio
88.1 FM
Crystal Radio
98 FM
Carlow Local Radio
99 FM
Coast 103
103 FM
C.C. Radio
90.25 FM
Capitol
93.75 FM
Centre Radio
101.5 FM
County Sounds Radio
98.5 FM

Double R Radio
1034 AM
Drogheda Community Radio
Drimnagh District Local Radio
1359 AM
Dungarvan Community Radio
98.5
Dublin City Radio
Diamond Radio
Downtown Radio Dublin
Dollymount Community Radio
Dublin Community Radio
963 AM
Donegal Community Radio
103 FM

Downtown Radio
88 FM
Dundrum Community Radio
94.8 FM
Diamond 106
106.1 FM

Emerald Radio
Eastside Radio
1308 AM
Became ERI
Eyre Radio Galway
East Coast Radio Rosslare
ERI
96.9 FM
Enniscorthy Local Radio
1512 AM
Election Radio '82
102 FM
Echo Radio
Erneside Radio
97.8 FM
Echo Community Radio
1071 AM

Fingal Community Radio
1575 AM
F41 Audio, Dublin

Glencoe Radio

Horizon FM
104 FM
Heartbeat
95.5 FM
H-Block Radio
Horizon Radio
88 FM
Hospital Radio, Dublin
97 FM
Hits 954
97.6 FM
Hometown Radio

Independent Radio Galway
Irish Christian Broadcast Service
981 AM
Island Radio
Independent Radio, Mayo.
101 FM

Kildare Community Radio
1401 AM
Kerry Local Radio
Kilkenny Community Radio
100 FM
KISS FM
102.7 FM
KISS FM
104.1/94.8 FM
KFM
95FM
Kildare Community Radio
1413 AM
KELO
KLAS 98 FM
98.5 FM
KLB Community Radio
103.9 FM
Kandy Radio
98 FM
KTOK FM
95.7 FM
KCR FM
106.25
Kiss FM
103.7
Kits 101 FM
100.9
Kingdom 102
102 FM

Laois Community Radio
102.1 FM
Limerick Community Radio
Leeside Community Radio
102 FM
Liberties Local Community Radio
104 FM
Leeside Radio
101.5
Longford Community Radio
1071 AM
Legan Local Radio
103.5 FM

Midleton Community Radio
96.9 FM
Midland Community Radio
1161 AM
Midland Radio Athlone
Mayo Community Radio
303 MW
Mid West Radio
Metro FM
Munster Broadcasting Company
96 FM

Mid-West Radio
1404 AM
Mid-Way Radio
98.7 FM
Mid-West Radio
87.9 FM
Music Power 96
96 FM

Northwest Radio
219 MW
Northern Radio
1314 AM
North Coast Local
North Side Radio
North Cork Local Radio
98 FM
Northwest Community Radio
98 FM
North Dublin Community Radio
105 FM
NRG 103
103 FM
Northern Star
999 AM
007 Radio

Premier Radio Dublin
Premier Radio International
Premier Atlantis Radio
Power 102
102.25
Power from Tullamore, Co. Offaly
Phoenix Radio
94.15 FM
Phoenix Radio
Pulsar 98
98.8

Q102
102 FM

Radio Clonmel
Radio Leinster
738 AM
Radio Carousel
Dundalk 1125 AM
North 1260 AM
Navan 1386 AM
Radio City
257 MW
Radio North East.
Radio Snowflake
99 FM
Radio Dublin
104.8 FM
Radio Dundalk

Radio Limerick Weekly Echo
Radio Nova
88 FM
Radio South County
963 AM
Radio Sandymount
1332 AM
Radio West
Radio Carlow
1413 AM
Radio Carol Ann
1125 AM
Radio O'Moore
Rainbow Radio
Radio North East
Radio Tralee Community
96 FM
Radio 257
257 MW
Radio West
999 AM
Radio Luimni
981 AM
Royal County Dublin
946 AM
Radio Sligo
1260 AM
Radio North West
1618 AM
Radio Dublin Channel 2
1250 AM
Radio Antrim
1395 AM
Radio Liberties
Radio Quad
Radio Belfield
Radio an Phobal
Radio na Saoirse
Radio Seagull
Radio Saor Chonamara
Ringsend Radio
Radio Breffni
Radio West
94.7 FM
Radio Luimnighe
96.4 FM
Radio Central
103.8 FM
Radio Charisma
98.2
Radio Caroline
98.8 FM
Radio na nGael
1350 AM
Radio Nova
98.2
Radio Ballyvaughn
Radio Woodquay

Radio North
96.1 FM
Rainbow Radio
96 FM
Ranelagh Community Radio
Radio Tower
107.9 FM
Radio Vera International

Sunshine Radio
100.5 FM
South City Radio
1314 AM
South Coast Radio
1557 AM
Southern Independent Radio
89 FM
South West Radio Dublin
Sonic Independent Radio Dublin
Skull and Crossbones Radio System
926 AM
Shannonside Community Radio
97.9 FM
Smile FM
94.15
Stereo Radio Munster
96.2
Signal Stereo 102
Sunshine Radio Cork
96 FM
Signal FM
96 FM
Sligo Radio
98.2
Southside 95
94.9 FM
Southside Radio
104 FM

Treble TR
97.5 FM
Tipperary Community Radio
99.9 FM
Telstar Community Radio
88.3 FM
Tallaght Community Radio
91.8 FM
The Sound Channel
98.7 FM
Channeling its sound into Limerick City
3CR
Twigs FM
98.5 FM

UCR 96 FM
United Ireland Radio

Viking 105

West Coast Community Radio
1152 AM
Waterford Local Radio
1197 AM
Westside Radio Dublin
1035 AM
Wicklow Local Radio
1359 AM
Wicklow Community Radio
Western Alternative Broadcasting
Corporation
Westside Radio
WKRC
WKLR
Wicklow Regatta Radio
Weekend Music Radio
Waterford Local Radio
88.9 FM
WBEN
98 FM
West Cork Local Radio
98 FM
Wonderland Radio
1359 AM
WSPD
105 FM
WRKY
103.3 FM
WCLR
103.4 FM
West Coast Radio
1413 AM
WKLR
98 FM
West Coast Radio
96.4 FM
Westside Radio
97.5 FM
WABC
106 FM

Zoom 103
Zee 103
FM only station in Omeath, Co.
Zee 100
96.1 FM

All the stations below belong to the first wave of Irish pirate radio. These were hobby stations. Many of these names refer to the same station, most only broadcast for a limited period of time. It is best to consult the main text for more information

Radio Melissa
Radio Melinda
Radio 66 operated by Jack O'Carroll
Radio Vanessa
Radio Romeo
Radio Valerie operated by Dermot Blake
Radio Santa Monica
Radio Blachliathe - Ken Sheehan's *original* Radio Dublin
Radio Northside operated by John Ryan
Radio 200
Radio Laxey
Radio Galaxy - all operated by Tony Boylan
Radio Karina
Radio Caroline - Cork
Radio Caroline - Dublin - from Billy Ebrill's house in Dalkey
Radio Eamo operated by Eamon McGovern
Radio Empathy - Ed McDowell's first station that tried to outgrow the hobby stage
Railway Road Radio - from Dublin's Inchicore
Radio Pandora
Radio City - this one from Crumlin
Radio Mi Amigo
Radio Monkstown

K.L.A.S. 98.5 FM

 Dublin's Only Easy Listening Station
...24 Hours a Day...

Schedule

Monday - Friday

8 am - 12 pm	Brian Craig
12 pm - 4 pm	Dan O'Sullivan Chat Show
4 pm - 8 pm	David Hynes
8 pm - 12 Midnight	Keith Shanley
Midnight —	Automatic

Saturday

8 am - 12 pm	Mike Swan
12 pm - 2 pm	John May 'Matters of the Heart'
2 pm - 6 pm	Dan O'Sullivan 'Sport'
6 pm - 9 pm	David Baker
9 pm —	Automatic

Sunday

8 am - 12 pm	Mike Swan
12 pm - 3 pm	Ian Turner
3 pm - 6 pm	Bryan Lambert
6 pm - 9 pm	David Baker
9 pm —	Automatic

SUNSHINE 101

Dublin City's
No. 1 Radio Station

Advertisement

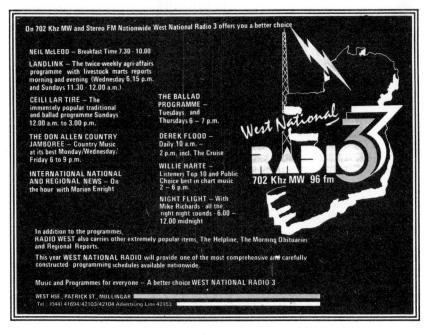